The Ultimate
HEART
HEALTHY
Full-Flavor Meal Plan

28-DAY
MEAL
PLAN

LOW-SODIUM MENUS, SHOPPING LISTS, TIPS + MORE TO HELP YOUR HEART!

Prevention

Photographs by Ted Cavanaugh: 128; Beatriz da Costa: 132; Chris Court: 134; Andrew De Santis: 10-11; Mike Garten: 62, 63, 68, 72, 84, 85, 100, 103, 105, 115, 123, 126, 130, 133, 137, 138, 141, 142, 143; Steve Giralt: 135; Raymond Hom: 67, 71, 99; Erika Lapresto: 61, 83, 119, 131, 140; Kate Mathis: 88, 116; Danielle Occhiogrosso Daly: 64, 82, 86, 87, 117, 127; Con Poulos: 98, 126; Armando Rafael: 99; Emily Kate Roeme: 129; Christopher Testani: 120; The Vorhees: 6-7; Jonny Valiant: 102; Anna Williams: 101; **Adobe Stock:** aamulya: 18; Alexandr Vorobev: 5; amnarj2006: 31; Atlas: 26 (avocado); baibaz: 25 (broccoli); Bozena Fulawka: 26 (garlic); galitskaya: 38 (hands); Jacob Lund: 46; Jira: 32; Jiri Hera: 47; Krafla: 30; lvnl: 9 (brain health); Mara Zemgaliete: 22; MarekPhotoDesign.com: 42; mizina: 33; nadianb: 17 (plate); nataliazakharova: 25 (leafy greens); Natika: 25 (tomatoes); New Africa: 25 (sweet pot), 28-29; Pixel-Shot: 9 (dog); rasilja: 26 (barley); Rawpixel.com: 36-37; ricka_kinamoto: 35; Sanja: 40-41; sonyakamoz: 24; valentinamaslova: 19; Wayhome Studio: 9 (woman stress); yolya_ilyasova: 27; **Getty Images:** burwellphotography/E+: 26 (turmeric); d3sign/Moment: 43; Eugene Mymrin/Moment: 12; Francesco Vaninetti Photo/Moment: 27 (outside); Jose Luis Pelaez Inc/DigitalVision: 20; Sangsiripech Tunruen/EyeEm: 25 (beans); SEAN GLADWELL/Moment: 25 (berries); Sommai Larkjit/EyeEm: 38 (plate); stockcam/E+: 17 (pretzel); The Good Brigade/DigitalVision: 27 (stretch); Tim Robberts/Stone: 8 (scale); Getty Images/Cavan Images RF: 15; Getty Images/Tetra images RF: 27, 45; Leo Patrizi: 14

Book design by Lauren Vitello

Recipes by Karen Ansel, RDN, Catherine Lo, Kate Merker, Colleen Montgomery, Nicole Papantoniou, The Good Housekeeping Test Kitchen, The Prevention Test Kitchen, Woman's Day Kitchen

Library of Congress Cataloging-in-Publication Data is on file with the publisher.

ISBN 978-1-955710-05-3

Printed in China

2 4 6 8 10 9 7 5 3 1 hardcover

H E A R S T

Table of Contents

Introduction: Heal Your Heart With Food 4

Chapter 1: Start Caring for Your Heart 6

Chapter 2: The Heart-Healthy Diet 28

Chapter 3: How to Use This Book 40

Chapter 4: 28-Day Meal Plan 48
Week 1 50
Week 2 73
Week 3 89
Week 4 106

Chapter 5: Bonus Recipes 124

Breakfast
Pumpkin Chocolate-Chip Oatmeal 52
Sweet Potato Toast with Yogurt and Berries 56
Green Berry Smoothie Bowl 59
Overnight Blueberry Oats 60
Mashed Sweet Potato Bowl 76
Skillet Berry French Toast 84
Spicy Veggie Saute 87
Apple Chia Pudding 93
Chocolate Protein Smoothie 94
Citrus-Pineapple Bowl 98
Zucchini Bread Overnight Oats 109
Open-Faced Avocado Sandwich 118
Smoothie Bowls 126
Very Berry Quinoa Muffins 126
Apple-Oatmeal Muffins 127
Chocolate-Cherry Granola Bars 128
Pumpkin-Cherry Breakfast Cookies 129

Lunch
Veggie Sandwich 53
Vegetable Fried Rice 61
Speedy Black Beans and Rice 76
Tomato Bean Stuffed Potato 93
Smashed Chickpea Salad Sandwich 108
Peach, Tomato, and Basil Salad 130
Smoky Chicken Soup 131
Marinated Summer Squash Salad 132
Warm Roasted Cauliflower and Spinach Salad 133
Chickpea, Spinach, and Quinoa Patties 133

Dinner
Tomato and Basil Spaghetti 62
Sweet and Sticky Tofu 64
Soba Salad with Chicken 67
Spring Green Panzanella 68
Butternut Squash and White Bean Soup 71

Air Fryer Mediterranean Chicken Bowls 72
Salmon with Citrusy Lentil Salad 82
Chickpea Curry 83
Creamy Vegan Linguine with Wild Mushrooms 85
Tofu Pad Thai 86
Spiced Cod with Rice Noodle Salad 87
Lemon-Marinated Herb Pasta Salad 88
Slow Cooker Butternut Squash Stew 99
Smoky Vegan Black Bean Soup 100
Roasted Cumin Shrimp and Asparagus 101
Balsamic Chicken with Apple, Lentil, and Spinach Salad 102
Pressure Cooker Winter Squash and Lentil Stew 103
BBQ Chickpea and Grilled Nectarine Salad 105
Supergreen Mushroom & Orzo Soup 115
Three-Bean Salad 116
Sheet Pan Chicken Fajitas 117
Pesto Pasta 118
Spicy Tofu Tacos 119
Halibut with Potatoes and Brussels Sprouts 120
Fiery Black Bean Soup 123
Cod with Crispy Green Beans 134
Zesty Shrimp with Chimichurri Rice 135
Everything Bagel Crusted Salmon with Herby Fennel Salad 137
Roasted Chili-Lime Drumsticks 138
Sticky Chicken with Scallion and Corn Rice 140

Sides
Garlic Ginger Sautéed Spinach 76
Steamed Broccoli 81
Classic Quinoa 97
Spicy Rice 109
Lemon Garlic Spinach 110
Rice and Pinto Beans 112
Savory Sautéed Kale 114
Roasted Sweet-and-Sour Brussels Sprouts 141
Potato Salad with Red Onion Vinaigrette 141
Carrot and Radish Salad 142
White Bean and Cucumber Salad 143
Turmeric-Roasted Beets With Orange Bell Pepper Romesco 143

Snacks
Honeydew with Cinnamon Yogurt Dip 49
Chocolate Hummus with Strawberries 59
Very Berry Bean Smoothie 60
Yellow Split Pea Dip 63
Smoky Roasted Chickpeas 77
Strawberry Banana Nice Cream 78
Banana Bread Smoothie 92
Cherry Chocolate Nice Cream 93
Chili Lime Roasted Chickpeas 97
Dairy-Free Tzatziki with Broccoli 97
Citrus-Pineapple Bowl 98
Vegan Queso 99
Garlic White Bean Dip with Sliced Cucumber 110

Heal Your Heart With Food

About a month into my maternity leave, I visited the cardiac rehab clinic where I had worked for the past 10 years. The very first face I saw? A 40-something-year-old patient of mine who, the last time we met, was struggling with ongoing chest pain, medication changes, and feelings of failure because no one could figure out why heart procedures couldn't keep his symptoms from worsening.

"I DID IT!" he said, exuberant. "I switched to a more plant-based diet like we discussed, and all of my symptoms are gone. I feel amazing!"

But he didn't need to say a word for me to notice the changes. A few weeks earlier, cardiac patients 30 years his senior were moving faster than he could on a recumbent bike. Any exertion caused him to huff, puff, and drip with sweat. Now, right after a workout, he was still sweaty but glowing, breathing normally, and ready for more.

The moment we talked, I realized there was a better way to help people struggling with heart problems. See, the current standard approach to heart disease—or more specifically, coronary artery disease (the most common form of heart disease that causes heart attacks)—focuses primarily on avoiding disease. This translates to cutting out foods and habits that contribute to the development of heart disease, taking medications to manage high blood pressure and cholesterol, and having procedures like stents and open-heart surgery.

This emphasis on treating signs and symptoms with medications and procedures—without considering and addressing the underlying causes—never sat well with me, and these feelings intensified as the years went by.

Don't get me wrong: Medications and heart procedures can be lifesaving. Unfortunately, though, I'd seen many of my patients fail using this approach.

"Maybe we need to flip the switch," I thought. Let's stop "avoiding disease" and start focusing on adopting lifestyle habits that promote healthy hearts and fulfilling lives. Overwhelming evidence shows that heart disease is largely preventable and, in some cases, reversible. Yet almost none of my heart patients knew this. So I decided to start a health coaching business that combines the most effective behavior change techniques with the heart-healthiest diet on the planet.

To supplement my master's degree in clinical exercise physiology and my work in cardiac rehabilitation, I obtained various certifications, including plant-based nutrition and several types of health and wellness coaching. I then created

my business, Wellness Within LLC, with the goal of helping people prevent chronic diseases (like heart disease and hypertension) that are heavily influenced by lifestyle factors, namely exercise and diet.

My clients are sick of managing their medications and a growing list of heart-related problems. Instead, they desire to take control of their health and proactively move toward feeling great again. And they can. Heart problems are not inevitable: Even heart attacks are preventable 90% of the time. What's more, even after heart problems develop, you still have the capacity to dramatically improve your heart health.

The number 1 risk factor for death is "dietary risks," according to the comprehensive Global Burden of Disease Study. In other words, what you eat has the biggest effect on your health. This is empowering! You can single-handedly control the most important and impactful influence on your health, even if you think it's too late.

With the help of this book, you have the chance to make small, realistic changes every day that, over time, add up to a huge positive impact on your heart health. This control lies in the greatly underestimated medicinal value of simple lifestyle choices like eating health-promoting foods, moving more, and nurturing your emotional health. You won't just see how your heart health improves, you will feel the difference.

Along the way, enjoy the ride, move at your own pace, and remember: You've got this.

In good health,

Colleen Montgomery, MS, CHWC, ACSM-CEP

CHAPTER 1

START CARINGFOR YOUR HEART

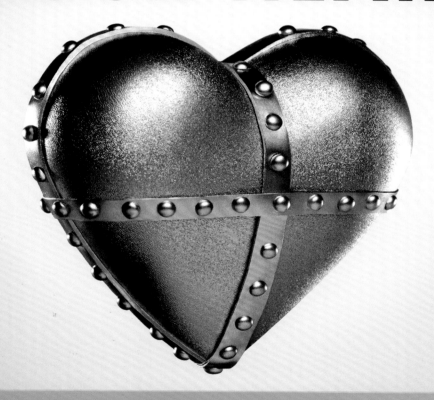

W hether you're in good health or you were recently diagnosed with a cardiac issue, the right time to begin focusing on heart health is now.

A whopping 80% of cardiovascular disease, including heart disease and stroke, can be prevented through lifestyle changes and proper screening. The key here is taking risk factors such as high cholesterol and physical inactivity seriously and getting them in check before they have the chance to snowball into a bigger problem.

And even after a heart attack or surgery, you can do so much to prevent your condition from progressing. Many people with serious heart issues who make the right lifestyle changes continue to thrive decades later.

The bottom line: Whatever your situation, you have the power to live a fulfilling, active, healthy life that supports your heart.

Why Heart Health Matters

You know your heart is vital, but you may not realize all that this organ does for you.

It's a pump: The heart sends blood through a network of blood vessels called the cardiovascular system. From there, the blood travels to every inch of your body.

Here's How Your Heart Works

1 Oxygen-depleted blood travels from the veins into the **right atrium.** This chamber then pumps the blood into the right ventricle.

2 The **right ventricle** squeezes the blood into the lungs to replenish it with oxygen and remove carbon dioxide.

3 The oxygen-rich blood then travels from the lungs into the **left atrium.** This chamber contracts and sends the blood into the left ventricle.

4 The strongest of the four chambers, the **left ventricle** pumps oxygenated blood out to the rest of the body via the arteries to provide oxygen and nutrients to our vital organs and muscles.

It's an electrical system: Our houses receive a constant supply of electricity to power up lights and appliances at any time. Similarly, electricity is constantly flowing through your heart: It begins at the top of the heart in the right atrium and spreads down and throughout the organ, powering each beat.

It's a muscle: One with incredible strength and endurance. The heart needs to pump blood nonstop through a vast network of blood vessels that feeds every inch of your body. The heart meets this demand with precision, supplying the exact oxygen and nutrients each body part needs to function every moment.

The Two-Way Wellness Street

As impressive as it is, the human heart isn't a solo act. It relies on the wellness of the rest of the body to function optimally, and vice versa. Here are just a few of the ways this relationship plays out. **Your heart health affects these four crucial parts of your life.**

1. Weight

Being an unhealthy weight can burden the heart. Carrying excess pounds increases the risk of insulin resistance, high blood pressure, high cholesterol, and low-grade systemic inflammation. Each of these conditions can increase your odds of developing blockages, called plaque, inside the blood vessels. If the heart can't work hard enough to pump blood past these blockages, the plaque can build up, further raising the risk of heart disease or a heart attack.

Cardiovascular health and healthy weight are interconnected. If you aren't as fit as you could be, you'll have less energy—and with less energy, you'll be less likely to even want to move. The result? You burn fewer calories. If you don't offset this by eating less, you gain weight. More weight leads to less energy, and the cycle continues. Luckily, you can break this cycle and turn it into an upward spiral by committing to small daily goals such as those to the right.

7 Quick and Easy Ways to Move More

Every chance to move—from walking a block to climbing a set of stairs— is an opportunity to burn calories, boost energy, and support a healthy weight. Take advantage of these and other moments:

1. Ditch the elevator—take the stairs every time.

2. At home, before going upstairs, do 5 to 10 incline pushups with your hands on the fourth or fifth step.

3. When getting up from watching TV, stand up from the couch, then sit back down. Repeat this 10 times.

4. Do walking lunges as you travel from one room in your house to another.

5. March in place or take a walk while talking on the phone.

6. Have a desk job? Set an alarm to remind you to stand up and stretch every 30 to 40 minutes. Even 3 to 5 minutes will do wonders.

7. Go for a walk after dinner. Aim for 10 minutes or more. Bonus: This helps with digestion.

2. Stress

Tending to your emotions and caring for your heart go hand in hand.

When you experience stress or other negative emotions, your heart kicks into high gear as blood pressure and heart rate increase. This physical response can be lifesaving if you are in danger, but most of our modern-day stress doesn't warrant such an intense reaction. And if your body undergoes this physical response multiple times a day for several years, it can increase day-to-day blood pressure, inflammation, and the chances of a heart attack. Worse, stress doesn't stand alone. It can lead to anger, hostility, and depression, all of which also increase the risk of heart disease.

On the flip side, when the heart isn't doing too well, we may respond in an emotional way. After a heart attack or open heart surgery, it's common to experience anxiety and depression.

3. Sleep

Not only do you feel great after a good night's sleep, your heart loves it too. When you slumber, your heart rate and blood pressure decrease, providing your heart with well-deserved rest. In fact, getting a healthy amount of sleep can mitigate heart attack risk despite a genetic predisposition. On the other hand, inadequate or fragmented sleep can increase blood pressure and insulin resistance, and six hours of sleep or less can increase the chances of a heart attack by 20%.

Sleep deprivation can further harm your heart by contributing to weight gain. Too little slumber increases appetite and cravings, leaves you tired and less likely to engage in physical activity, and hinders your ability to cope with everyday stressors. Instead, you may stress-eat sweets and potentially add pounds.

4. Brain Health

Brain health and heart health have many commonalities. For example, the poor eating habits that can cause a heart attack can also lead to a stroke, because both conditions stem from damaged blood vessels. Additionally, the heart and brain are strongly connected in an emotional sense. Wear and tear on the mind can show up as everything from a racing heartbeat to a very real condition called broken heart syndrome.

Simply put, to care for the heart is to care for the brain. Eat well, move more, and tend to your emotional well-being, and your chances of heart problems, stroke, vascular dementia, and even Alzheimer's disease collectively decrease.

What Is Your Heart Telling You?

"If you listen to your body when it whispers, you won't have to hear it scream."

Have you heard this saying? It couldn't be more true when it comes to heart health. If you don't provide your heart with the right nutrients or opportunity to exercise, it might speak to you, growing increasingly louder until you heed its signals.

A heart's whisper often first appears in the form of a nondescript symptom that could be mistaken for something else. Whispers include:

- A general decrease in energy level

- Taking longer to do normal physical activity, such as walking or other exercise

- Increasing difficulty completing normal daily tasks, such as household chores

Sometimes the whisper is a little louder and more serious. These more pronounced symptoms could include:

- Pain or discomfort in your chest, including feelings of pressure, squeezing, heaviness, tightness, burning, or fullness

- Pain or discomfort in your upper back, jaw, neck, throat, one or both arms, or stomach area

- New or worsening shortness of breath with exertion or even at rest

- Indigestion, nausea, or vomiting

- Lightheadedness or dizziness

- Extreme fatigue

Though these whispers may not be your heart, do not ignore them. For one, doing so could lead to more limiting symptoms, including more severe and frequent chest discomfort or shortness of breath. For another, a heart attack could be looming. This happens when the heart isn't getting enough blood, usually due to blockage in an artery. Heart attacks can be small, or they can lead to disability or death.

If heart attack symptoms are caught in time, damage can be minimized. For example, a surgeon may place a stent in the affected artery to reopen the blood vessel and restore blood flow. Or they may perform coronary artery bypass graft (CABG) surgery, in which arteries from the legs or arms are harvested and sutured to the heart muscle to bypass diseased blood vessels. These procedures can be lifesaving, but they do not address or correct the root causes of heart disease. The disease can and often does continue to progress—causing more blockages and possible recurrence of heart attacks or heart procedures—unless you begin to make lifestyle changes.

Furthermore, heart disease can eventually evolve into heart failure, in which the heart can no longer pump efficiently enough to keep up with the body's demands. People with heart failure are often severely symptomatic and limited in their daily activities. They are at higher risk for sudden cardiac arrest, depression, and overall poor quality of life.

What can you do about it?

Always listen to the whispers. Doing so early gives you the power to address what is going on and reignites your chances of living a very healthy and vibrant life.

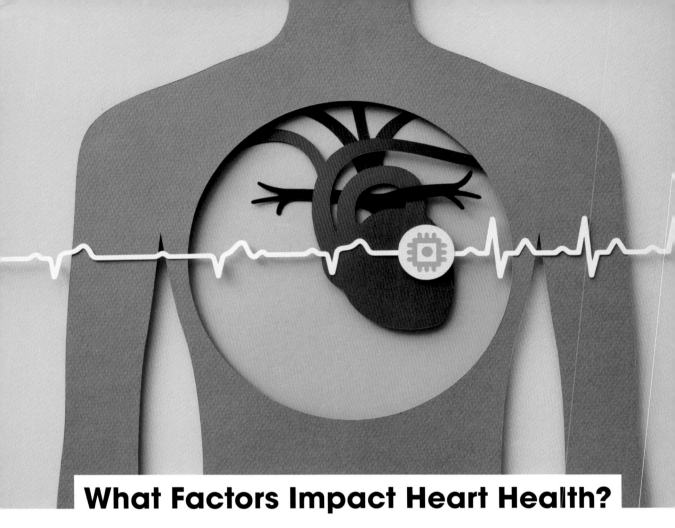

What Factors Impact Heart Health?

Many things play a role in heart health, and these variables fall into two categories:

1. **Non-modifiable risk factors**
While these are not within your control, being aware of them can improve your understanding of your overall risk for heart problems.

2. **Modifiable risk factors**
Most of what affects your heart health is modifiable, or within your control.

Let's take a closer look at the different risk factors that affect your heart health.

Non-Modifiable: Genetics

As with most health conditions, a family history of heart problems can increase your own risk. This is true if you have a:

♂ **Male parent, sibling, or child who developed heart problems** (heart attack, angioplasty or stent procedure, open-heart surgery, heart failure, or sudden cardiac death) before age 55, and/or

♀ **Female parent, sibling, or child who developed heart problems** before age 65

Be heart smart. Even if you have a genetic predisposition to heart disease, lifestyle factors influence the way your genes act. When you engage in healthy behaviors, it appears that you have the ability to "turn off" the genes that would otherwise raise your risk. That's right: Simply following the advice mentioned throughout this book may help keep these particular genes at bay. Need proof? The INTERHEART study of 30,000 people showed that nine modifiable lifestyle factors accounted for a whopping 90% of heart attacks in men and 94% of heart attacks in women.

Non-Modifiable: Age

Age largely impacts heart health because more years on earth provides more opportunity to engage in unhealthy behaviors. Though heart disease can happen at any age, your gender determines when your risk increases.

Men: Heart disease risk increases after 45. In general, men of any age have a higher risk of heart disease compared to women.

Women: Risk increases after 55, as menopause causes a number of biological changes that can impact heart health.

Be heart smart. Despite our eternal search for the fountain of youth, aging is unavoidable. Luckily, the tips and tools sprinkled throughout this book emphasize actions that have a clear positive impact on heart health, no matter your age.

Modifiable: Smoking

Smoking gives you two to four times higher risk of developing coronary artery disease, the most common form of heart disease. That's because smoking damages blood vessels throughout the body. In particular, smoking can stiffen and thicken the walls of the coronary arteries, which supply the heart with blood and oxygen. As a result, blood pressure increases, making your heart work harder. Your heart also has to work faster because smoking increases heart rate.

Unfortunately, that's not all. Smoking reduces HDL cholesterol, the "good" type that protects the heart. Lastly, this habit increases the risk of developing blood clots, which can cause a heart attack.

Be heart smart. If you don't smoke, avoid secondhand smoke, which can raise the risk of developing heart disease by 25% to 30%. Even 30 minutes of exposure can injure blood vessels.

If you do smoke, there's good news: After quitting and remaining smoke-free for 10 years, your risk of heart disease returns to that of a non-smoker. That said, it's not unusual to take a few tries to successfully quit. Don't ever give up, and find support. Talk to your doctor about prescription medication and over-the-counter nicotine replacement options, consider support groups, and check out:

- **Smokefree.gov**
- **1-800-QUIT-NOW (1-800-784-8669)**
- **quitSTART app**

Modifiable: Physical Inactivity

Sitting for four or more total hours or for frequent 30-minute stints throughout the day can increase heart disease risk. If you're not moving, you're not burning calories or using blood sugar to fuel the body. This can increase arterial stiffness, raising your risk of heart disease as well as many of its related risk factors, including type 2 diabetes and high blood pressure. Even if you exercise regularly, prolonged sitting can result in poor health outcomes. Luckily, small bursts of movement can have a big impact on your heart.

Be heart smart. Every little step truly counts. Squeeze movement in whenever you can (and remember to talk to your doctor before starting any exercise program).

- Aim for 30 minutes or more of cardiovascular exercise almost every day. If it's easier, do three 10-minute sessions.

- New to exercise? Start with 5 to 10 minutes of cardio, like walking or swimming, three or four times a week. Gradually add another day and more time per session until you hit 20 to 30 minutes or more five to seven days weekly.

- Add resistance exercises to your day. Do squats while brushing your teeth or pushups against the wall while your coffee brews. Aim for 10 reps at least twice a day.

- Shorten periods of prolonged sitting by moving: Stand up for 1 to 5 minutes at least once or twice every hour.

Exercise Is Medicine

Exercise is so powerful that after just one session of at least 10 minutes, you can:

- Flood your body with anti-inflammatory hormones (inflammation is a key driver in poor blood vessel health and the development of heart disease)

- Lower your blood pressure for up to 13 hours

- Increase insulin sensitivity for up to 48 hours

- Improve mood and decrease stress

Stick to it, and long-term activity helps your heart even more. It can:

- Reduce inflammation, resting blood pressure, heart rate, and triglycerides

- Help decrease weight and belly fat

- Improve blood sugars and insulin sensitivity

- Help make blood less "sticky," which improves circulation

- Help manage depression and anxiety

- Improve the chances of survival after a heart attack

Best Exercise for Heart Health

The best exercise for your heart is the type of exercise you'll do the most! Remember, every single time you move counts. Here are some simple ways to get started:

1. DANCING Shaking your groove thing gets your heart pumping, strengthening it while also lifting your mood. And you don't even feel like you're exercising!

2. WALKING The most accessible and practical form of exercise, walking is free and can be done right outside your front door. And guess what? The ultimate steps-per-day goal is not 10,000. A less intimidating and more attainable 7,500 steps is linked with a lower death rate. You can do more steps if you want to, but the additional benefit to your heart may remain at the same level.

3. CHAIR EXERCISES Physical activity is always possible, even if you lack energy or are experiencing joint pain. While sitting, pretend to climb a rope, raise your arms out to the side and over your head, or try chair yoga. Breaking up sitting time with creative seated exercises can counteract the negative effects of being sedentary.

4. BODYWEIGHT EXERCISES
Because muscle burns more calories at rest than fat, increasing muscle mass can aid in weight loss. Moves like lunges, squats, or wall pushups can be done anywhere and don't require any equipment.

5. MINI EXERCISE BIKE One of the most important things you can do to improve heart health is to break the habit of being sedentary. A mini exercise bike (a small, por- table machine that can be placed at the base of a chair or couch) is a unique way to move while sitting. It's portable, inexpensive, and can be used almost anywhere while you're sitting down.

6. MIIT Moderate-intensity interval training combines short intervals of moderate-intensity exercise (such as brisk walking or light jogging) with periods of rest or low-intensity exercise (such as slow walking). Intervals effectively increase cardiovascular fitness. And the greater your cardiovascu- lar fitness, the lower your risk of heart problems.

Understand Your Blood Pressure Reading

- **Systolic Blood Pressure (top number):** measures the amount of force the heart exerts onto your blood vessel walls every time it beats.

- **Diastolic Blood Pressure (bottom number):** measures the amount of force the heart exerts onto the blood vessel walls in between heart beats.

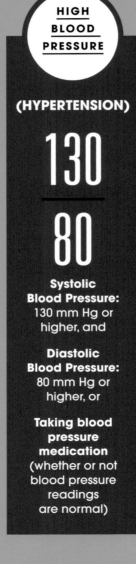

OPTIMAL BLOOD PRESSURE

120
80

Systolic Blood Pressure: 120 mm Hg or less, and

Diastolic Blood Pressure: 80 mm Hg or less

HIGH BLOOD PRESSURE (HYPERTENSION)

130
80

Systolic Blood Pressure: 130 mm Hg or higher, and

Diastolic Blood Pressure: 80 mm Hg or higher, or

Taking blood pressure medication (whether or not blood pressure readings are normal)

Modifiable: High Blood Pressure

Blood pressure is the amount of pressure inside your heart and blood vessels. About 5% to 10% of high blood pressure is due to an underlying condition or certain medication. The vast majority of people, however, develop hypertension due to some combination of diet, weight, physical inactivity, and other factors.

Food is a big player. The standard fat- and salt-rich American diet damages blood vessels and inhibits them from precisely dilating and contracting.

A high-fat meal, especially one high in saturated fat, can spike blood pressure in a few ways. First, meals rich in fat can stiffen and constrict blood vessels. Second, saturated fat makes blood thicker and stickier, causing the heart to work harder to pump that blood. Third, saturated fat appears to inhibit HDL from keeping "bad" LDL cholesterol in check. So if you consume three high-fat meals a day, your blood pressure is compromised a majority of every day, simply due to what you eat.

In terms of salt, the body tightly regulates sodium levels. When you eat high-sodium foods like salty snacks and processed meats, the sodium concentration in your blood rises above desired levels. In response, your body retains water in an effort to dilute the sodium concentration. The result? You end up with a greater volume of blood in your blood vessels, therefore raising blood pressure.

It's important to have your blood pressure checked regularly because hypertension usually doesn't cause symptoms. Left untreated, it can lead to heart attack, heart failure, stroke, dementia, eye damage, and kidney failure.

Be heart smart There is so much you can do to improve blood pressure. And the higher your blood pressure is, the more likely it is to respond to the healthy changes that you make. Here are three effective places to start:

1. SWAP OUT SATURATED FAT

Choosing healthier alternatives has been shown to be more effective than reaching for lean and low-fat versions of our main saturated fat sources. Take it from the "Blue Zones," the five locations around the world (including Sardinia, Italy, and Okinawa, Japan) where people live the longest and enjoy low rates of high blood pressure and heart disease. Their diets center on unprocessed foods, which are typically low in saturated fat, and they have meat about five times per month on average.

The main sources of saturated fat in the U.S. diet include:

- Cheese, milk, butter, and margarine
- Beef and processed meats such as sausages and lunch meat
- Coconut and palm oils
- Baked goods such as cakes, cookies, pastries, and pies
- Chicken and turkey
- Processed foods such as crackers, popcorn, and chips

See "Heart-Healthy Food Swaps" (page 39) for healthier options.

2. REDUCE SALT INTAKE

About 75% of the sodium in our diets comes from restaurant and processed foods, so taking it easy with the salt shaker at home can make a meaningful dent. This is where neuroplasticity, or the brain's ability to change, comes in. Neuroplasticity plays a role when your taste buds adapt to and even learn to love new flavors. As you gradually reduce how much salt you cook with and add to meals, over time you may prefer less-salty food.

3. PACK YOUR MENU WITH BLOOD PRESSURE-FRIENDLY FOODS

Nitrates, potassium, magnesium, vitamin C, and folate help blood vessels repair and retain their flexibility, in turn keeping blood pressure at healthy levels. But rather than taking a supplement, eat whole foods. The nutrients in food work synergistically to provide your body with exactly what it needs to thrive.

Try adding the following to your meals, with the goal of including at least one or more of these nutrients in every meal:

- **Nitrates:** Spinach, arugula, Brussels sprouts, broccoli, asparagus, kale, cauliflower, beets
- **Potassium:** Oranges, white beans, leafy greens, grapes, potatoes, carrots, broccoli
- **Magnesium:** Avocados, almonds, chia seeds, tofu, legumes (beans, chickpeas, lentils, split peas), oats, quinoa, leafy greens, bananas
- **Vitamin C:** Citrus fruits, kiwi, berries, broccoli, Brussels sprouts, cauliflower, spinach, tomatoes, potatoes
- **Folate:** Broccoli, Brussels sprouts, beets, leafy greens, legumes, asparagus, citrus fruits, nuts, seeds

Modifiable: High Cholesterol

Cholesterol is a waxy substance that helps build cells. Your liver produces all the cholesterol your body needs. It's when you eat foods that elevate "bad" LDL cholesterol or lower "good" HDL cholesterol that you can begin to run into health problems.

LDL cholesterol plays a central role in the formation of plaques, or blockages, on the walls of the coronary arteries. If these blockages grow big enough, they can partially or fully obstruct the flow of blood.

Partial restriction means the heart might not receive as much blood as it needs and can temporarily cause symptoms like chest discomfort. Full restriction means blood flow is completely cut off to the heart, starving it of oxygen. This can lead to a heart attack. A heart attack can also occur if a piece of plaque breaks off from the blood vessel wall. A blood clot then forms in its place and can become large enough to block all blood from traveling around it.

Be heart smart Shifts in your diet and lifestyle can effectively help lower LDL cholesterol levels.

1. INCREASE FIBER

Fiber is a cholesterol-lowering powerhouse. Soluble fiber in particular binds to LDL cholesterol in your small intestine and removes it from your body through your feces.

Fiber is only found in plant-based foods. A list of fiber-rich foods that are particularly effective in lowering LDL cholesterol are found in the box to the right.

FIBER-RICH FOODS

- Oats
- Nuts, such as almonds
- Vegetables, such as Brussels sprouts, eggplant, and okra
- Soy, such as soybeans and tofu
- Wheat germ and wheat bran
- Beans
- Fruit, such as strawberries, citrus fruits, grapes, and apples
- Barley

2. REDUCE SATURATED FAT

Saturated fat triggers the liver to produce more cholesterol. To keep cholesterol levels in check, the American Heart Association recommends eating no more than 6% of your daily calories from saturated fat. For someone eating 2,000 calories per day, that's about 11 to 13 grams of saturated fat.

3. AVOID TRANS FAT

Man-made trans fat increases the shelf life of foods. This fat is especially harmful to the heart because it can both raise LDL cholesterol and lower HDL cholesterol.

Trans fat goes by the name "partially hydrogenated oil" when listed as an ingredient. This oil is most often found in:

- Fried foods such as french fries and doughnuts
- Shelf-stable foods like crackers, cookies, baked goods, pastries, pie crusts, and pizza crusts
- Stick margarine and shortening

No amount of trans fat is considered safe to eat. Trans fat is sneaky, so you need to not only check the nutrition facts for trans fats but also read the ingredients list to check for the words "partially hydrogenated." If a food contains less than 0.5 grams of trans fat per serving, that number is rounded down to zero on the label. It might not sound like much, but eating three servings of such a food or multiple foods per day can add up to higher cholesterol over time.

4. LIMIT DIETARY CHOLESTEROL

Don't be misled: Although our bodies only absorb some of the cholesterol that we eat, dietary cholesterol does raise blood cholesterol. And that can harm your heart: A 2019 study published in *JAMA* found that each 300-milligram (mg) intake of daily cholesterol was associated with a 17% increase in cardiovascular disease risk.

Cholesterol is produced in the liver, so cholesterol is found in animal foods and not in plant-based foods. The main dietary sources of cholesterol are:

CHOLESTEROL-RICH FOODS

- Eggs
- Seafood
- Beef and pork
- Poultry
- Cheese and butter

5. GET MOVING

Exercise's effect on cholesterol levels cannot be ignored. Aerobic exercise may help lower LDL cholesterol by about three to six points, while strength training may help lower LDL cholesterol and triglycerides by six to nine points. But time in the gym isn't the only thing that matters: A sedentary lifestyle is associated with lower HDL cholesterol.

See "Best Exercises for Heart Health" on page 15 for practical tips to start moving today, no matter your current fitness level or limitations. Even daily chores, like vacuuming or gardening, can help.

6. ACHIEVE A HEALTHY WEIGHT

Excess weight is a double whammy. It can raise LDL cholesterol as well as lower HDL cholesterol. Luckily, losing as little as 5% to 10% of your total body weight may improve cholesterol levels. For practical and effective tips to achieve a healthy weight for good, see "Excess Weight," page 22.

7. QUIT SMOKING

Smoking lowers HDL cholesterol levels. Quitting can reverse this and also dramatically lower the risk of heart disease.

Cholesterol by the Numbers

If you've ever had your blood cholesterol levels tested, you know that doctors tend to check total cholesterol, LDL, HDL, and sometimes triglycerides.

- **Triglycerides:** Although they're not a type of cholesterol, triglycerides are a similar type of fat that circulates in the blood and can raise the risk of heart disease.

- **Total cholesterol:** This number includes not only LDL and HDL, but also 20% of your triglycerides.

- **LDL:** Considered "bad" cholesterol, LDL deposits in areas of your body where it doesn't belong—such as the walls of your arteries—compromising blood flow and raising your risk for heart attack. Remember LDL cholesterol by the L: It's the "lousy" cholesterol or the number that you want to keep "low."

- **HDL:** Considered "good" cholesterol, HDL helps remove excess LDL cholesterol from areas of the body where it doesn't belong and bring it back to the liver. From there, it is excreted from the body. Hence, HDL lowers heart disease risk. Remember the H in HDL: It's the "healthy" cholesterol, or the number that you want to keep "high."

High cholesterol is defined as:

- LDL cholesterol > 130 mg/dL (<100 is desirable), or

- HDL cholesterol < 40 mg/dL in men or < 50 mg/dL in women, or

- Non-HDL cholesterol (total cholesterol minus HDL cholesterol) > 130 mg/dL, or

- Being on cholesterol-lowering medication, whether or not your numbers are normal

- If total cholesterol is the only measure available: > 200 mg/dL (the above values are more predictive of health problems than total cholesterol alone)

And high triglycerides is defined as:

- > 150 mg/dL

TOTAL CHOLESTEROL MG/DL

Desirable	Borderline High	High
	200	240

LDL CHOLESTEROL MG/DL

Optimal	Near Optimal	Borderline High	High	Very High
	100	130	160	190

HDL CHOLESTEROL MG/DL MALE

Undesirable	Acceptable	Optimal
	40	60

HDL CHOLESTEROL MG/DL FEMALE

Undesirable	Acceptable	Optimal
	50	60

NON-HDL CHOLESTEROL MG/DL

Desirable	Undesirable
	130

TRIGLYCERIDES MG/DL

Normal	Borderline High	High	Very High
	150	200	500

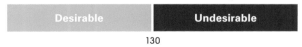

Modifiable: Excess Weight

Your heart has to work harder 24/7 to provide blood, oxygen, and nutrients to any additional body weight you carry. Worse, excess weight, especially in the midsection (a.k.a. belly fat), increases the risk of many conditions associated with heart disease, such as:

- High blood pressure
- High cholesterol
- Diabetes
- Systemic, low-grade inflammation
- Depression

Be heart smart Losing weight is no small feat. Luckily, rethinking how we typically approach losing weight can be refreshing and highly effective.

1. EAT SMARTER Restriction and hunger never work in the long run. So instead of focusing on eating less, aim to replace higher-calorie foods with lower-calorie ones.

I recommend choosing foods based on their calorie content per pound. People tend to have the most success in losing weight and maintaining a healthy weight when they eat mostly foods that have 600 or fewer calories per pound. These foods include (from lowest to highest calorie density) non-starchy vegetables, fruit, starchy vegetables, whole grains, and legumes such as beans and lentils. Foods that are more calorie dense and more likely to contribute to weight gain include (from lowest to highest calorie density) eggs, avocado, meat, bread and bagels, dairy, sugar, nuts and seeds, and oil of any kind, which contains an incredible 4,000 calories per pound.

Low-Calorie-Per-Pound Foods

FOOD	CALORIES/LB
Leafy greens	100
Bell peppers	100
Mushrooms	200
Apples	300
Potatoes	400
Oats	400
Brown rice	500
Pasta	500
Beans	600

2. FILL UP ON FIBER Fiber adds bulk to your meals and activates the stretch receptors in your stomach that tell your brain that the stomach is getting full. So stick with high-fiber foods, and you'll feel fuller, longer. Good choices include whole grains, vegetables, fruit, legumes, and nuts and seeds. Yes, I just said nuts and seeds are very calorie-dense, so be mindful of portion size if you are watching your weight.

3. USE THE 80% RULE People who reside in the Blue Zones, where people live longer, stop eating once they feel about 80% full. This prevents them from consuming unnecessary calories. To help with this, portion out a meal and eat as much as you want from that plate. Then, before you reach for seconds, take a break. Allow your stomach time to send a signal to your brain that you're full. This can take up to 20 minutes, so be patient and distract yourself. You may find that you start to feel full after a little bit and those leftovers can be saved, which saves you money.

4. MOVE MORE Diet alone leads to the loss of both fat and muscle mass. Adding exercise to your dietary changes can increase weight loss by about 20% while helping maintain muscle mass. This is key for losing pounds because muscle burns a lot of calories at rest.

With that said, formal exercise is not much good if you sit the rest of the day. You want to be physically active throughout the day to promote weight loss and better health. Remember, every single effort counts. Even walking into the bank instead of using the drive-through makes a difference.

Modifiable: Elevated Blood Sugars

Your body produces the hormone insulin to unlock cell doors and allow glucose (sugar) to move out of the blood and into cells where it's used as fuel. Insulin resistance occurs when the cells of the body don't respond appropriately to insulin, causing excess glucose to be trapped in the blood. The resulting elevated blood sugar levels can lead to prediabetes or type 2 diabetes.

Over time, excess blood sugar can damage the lining of blood vessels. This initiates the formation of plaque that can lead to a heart attack.

Be heart smart High blood glucose shouldn't be blamed on high carbohydrate consumption. Researchers have come to this conclusion from observing people with insulin resistance: When they consume carbs, their blood sugar levels spike sharply. But there's 100 years of research that confirm that a diet high in fat—saturated fat in particular—causes insulin resistance.

The best way to prevent the onset of prediabetes and type 2 diabetes is to stick to a heart-healthy diet centered predominantly on plant-based foods, like the one discussed in this book.

This diet may also help if you have diabetes. Study after study suggests that people living with type 2 diabetes can successfully treat and even reverse their condition by reducing saturated fat, increasing fiber, and restoring insulin sensitivity. (Refer to pages 17 and 18 to learn how you can lower saturated fat intake and boost fiber intake.)

As a bonus, any weight loss you experience also effectively reduces blood sugars and prevents prediabetes from progressing into type 2 diabetes. And don't forget exercise, another powerful way to lower blood sugar levels and reverse prediabetes.

4 NUMBERS FOR HEART HEALTH

BLOOD PRESSURE
WHAT IT IS: The force of your blood pressing against your artery walls

IDEAL GOAL: Less than 120/80 mm Hg

WHY: High blood pressure, defined as 130/80 mm Hg and above, increases your risk of strokes and heart attacks

BLOOD SUGAR
WHAT IT IS: The amount of sugar (or glucose) in your blood, measured by hemoglobin Alc and/or fasting blood glucose tests

IDEAL GOAL: HbAlc less than 5.7%; fasting glucose less than 126 mg/dL

WHY: Diabetes is diagnosed when HbAlc is 6.5% or higher and/or fasting glucose is 126 mg/dL or higher. Too-high sugar levels can damage blood vessels, making you more susceptible to heart disease.

BLOOD CHOLESTEROL
WHAT IT IS: A fat-like, waxy substance in the blood

IDEAL GOAL:

- Total cholesterol: Less than 200 mg/dL;
- Triglycerides: Less than 150 mg/dL;
- HDL Cholesterol: Greater than 60 mg/dL;
- Bad LDL cholesterol: less than 100 mg/dL

WHY: Higher levels of cholesterol may block blood flow to the heart.

BODY MASS INDEX
WHAT IT IS: A measure of body fat calculated using your height and weight

IDEAL GOAL: 18.5 to 24.9

WHY: Excess body weight (a BMI of 25 and above is considered overweight; 30 and above is considered obese) increases heart disease risk, especially when waist circumference goes up.

The Best Foods for Heart Health

Food is fundamental to preventing and managing almost every risk factor related to heart health. Your overall eating pattern matters most, and that's what we'll focus on in the next 28 days. Still, some foods are better for your ticker than others. Strive to fill your meals every day with as many of these heart-loving ingredients as you can.

1 LEAFY GREENS: Seven cups raw or 3½ cups cooked spinach, arugula, beet greens, kale, and other leafy greens a week has been shown to decrease risk of coronary heart disease by 67%. This is largely due to the high nitrate content, which heals blood vessels and helps them relax.

2 SWEET POTATOES: These taters are high in potassium, which helps blood vessels dilate and can decrease blood pressure.

3 FLAXSEED: This seed is known for its high heart-healthy omega-3 fat content, and two heaping tablespoons of ground flaxseed a day was shown to decrease systolic blood pressure by 15 points and diastolic blood pressure by 7 points in people with high blood pressure.

4 BEANS: Beans are loaded with fiber. In a study out of Harvard, just ⅓ cup beans daily was associated with a 38% reduction in heart attack risk.

5 OATMEAL: The simple change to eating 1½ cups of cooked oatmeal in the morning can, on average, reduce total cholesterol by 5% and LDL cholesterol by 7%.

6 BERRIES: These fruits appear to be a triple threat. Eating about 1 cup per day has been shown to increase "good" HDL cholesterol, decrease systolic blood pressure, and prevent platelets (a component of blood) from sticking together. Less sticky blood is easier for your heart to pump through your system.

7 BROCCOLI: This powerhouse cruciferous vegetable is a great source of potassium, nitrates, folate, and vitamin C, all of which proactively support healthy blood vessel function and healthy blood pressure.

8 WALNUTS: These nuts have been shown to lower "bad" LDL cholesterol and improve inflammation, insulin resistance, and blood vessel function. A little goes a long way, because walnuts are calorie dense. Stick to 1 ounce (about 12 to 14 walnut halves) a day.

9 TOMATOES: Inflammation plays an important role in blood vessel dysfunction and heart disease in general. Tomatoes are rich in lycopene, a powerful antioxidant that helps reduce inflammation. Cooked tomatoes are best, because heat increases the amount of lycopene available for your body to absorb.

10 TURMERIC: Herbs and spices are highly anti-inflammatory, and turmeric tops the list. Curcumin, a compound found in this spice, also protects against plaque formation inside blood vessels.

11 GARLIC: Embrace bad breath! Garlic can improve cholesterol and blood pressure, and just ¼ teaspoon garlic powder daily can boost blood vessel function.

12 DARK CHOCOLATE: In a review published in *BMJ* in 2011, people who consumed the highest amount of dark chocolate had a 37% reduction in cardiovascular disease compared to those who ate the least. The healthiest way to enjoy its antioxidant properties is to choose chocolate that contains at least 72% cocoa.

13 AVOCADOS: Known as "nature's mayo," avocados are an excellent source of monounsaturated fats, a healthy type of fat that helps lower LDL cholesterol. They also pack a big potassium punch.

14 BARLEY: Due to its high levels of a soluble fiber called beta-glucan, barley is one of the most effective cholesterol-lowering foods.

Be a Power Plant

Changing from a meat-heavy diet to a plant-based one doesn't have to happen overnight. Here are some fun and easy ideas to tip the balance in favor of your heart—and taste buds:

- Start with one plant-based meal per day. Breakfast is arguably the easiest, with simple stand-ins including chia pudding, avocado toast, or oatmeal with almond butter and berries.

- Add a handful of leafy greens to everything: pasta sauce, sandwiches, burrito bowls, etc.

- Try smoothies or smoothie bowls.

- Eat the rainbow. Strive to eat something red, orange/yellow, green, blue/purple, and even white (as in cauliflower or garlic, not bread or rice) every day.

- Eat 30 different types of plants a week. The largest study to date on the gut microbiome showed that this amount of variety gives your gut bacteria enough fiber and variety of nutrients to achieve great gut health. If 30 sounds like a lot, start with 10, and build from there.

- Take a favorite meal and search online for how to transform it into a delicious plant-based version. Keep trying different recipes and tweaking them until you have a meal you love.

5 THINGS YOU CAN DO RIGHT NOW *for your heart*

STRETCH

Stretching every morning can help reduce blood vessel stiffness, which can help improve blood pressure.

SET AN ALARM

Get 7–8 hours of sleep each night. This gives your cardiovascular system the reboot it needs to support a healthy blood pressure.

GO OUTSIDE

Spending 5 minutes in nature is the perfect antidote to stress. The first 5 minutes spent in nature seem to cause the biggest boost in mood.

STAND UP

Prolonged sitting stiffens blood vessels and negatively affects circulation. Find ways to get off your tush! Check emails standing at your kitchen counter, have phone conversations while walking the neighborhood or around your home, and march in place during TV commercials.

BREATHE

Paying attention to your breath is a powerful way to redirect your mind away from worries, focus on the present moment, and reduce stress. Try box breathing:

- Inhale for 4 seconds
- Hold your breath for 4 seconds
- Exhale for 4 seconds
- Hold your breath again for 4 seconds
- Repeat for 1–5 minutes

CHAPTER 2

THE HEART-HEALTHY DIET

Food truly is medicine, and the evidence is clear: The best eating style for your heart is a whole-foods, predominantly plant-based diet.

What Are Whole Foods?

Foods that are as close to their natural state as possible. In other words, they are minimally processed, like a whole potato versus potato chips. The less processed a food is, the more nutritious it is.

Defining Plant-Based

Eating a plant-based diet means that most of the time you eat foods that come from plants, such as vegetables, fruit, whole grains, nuts, and seeds. You can choose to reduce your meat and dairy intake, eat these foods once in a while, or eliminate them altogether.

This style of eating has been shown to prevent heart problems in big ways. One study published in the *Journal of the American Heart Association (JAHA)* in 2019 followed 12,000 people over the course of 29 years. The researchers concluded that those who ate diets rich in plant-based foods and low in animal-based foods had a 16% lower risk of cardiovascular disease and 32% lower risk of cardiovascular disease death.

Another *JAHA* study, published in 2021, came to the same conclusion: Following a predominantly plant-rich diet was associated with a significantly lower risk of heart disease. Again, you do not have to completely exclude animal-based foods to see these benefits, but you do need to heavily emphasize plant-based foods in your diet.

But it's not only about prevention. Older research suggests that following a plant-based diet may even reverse heart disease. That's right: The blockages inside the coronary arteries shrink, which may effectively prevent future heart attacks and open-heart surgery. No other way of eating has ever been shown to have such a profound impact on our hearts.

Before we go on, let me address some questions I'm frequently asked about this meal plan.

Q: Can I still eat meat, dairy, eggs, and processed foods?

A: You are in the driver's seat. If you wish to continue eating these foods, go ahead. You'll even see them sprinkled throughout the 28-day meal plan. Just know that the best heart health outcomes appear to occur when you eat these foods sparingly. To continue supporting your heart health:

- Limit red and processed meats as much as you are willing and able

- Prioritize low-fat or fat-free dairy over whole-fat dairy

- Prioritize egg whites over whole eggs

- Try to limit high-fat processed foods, especially ones that include tropical oils such as palm, palm kernel, and coconut oils, all of which are very high in saturated fat

Q: Will I meet all of my nutritional needs on a plant-based diet?

A: Compared to meat eaters, plant-based eaters generally have fewer nutrient deficiencies. It's true: people who eat a typical meat-heavy Western diet consume lower amounts of many nutrients, including fiber, vitamins C and E, magnesium, iodine, calcium, and folate.

One nutrient that cannot be obtained from plants is vitamin B_{12}. If at any point you decide to cut out animal foods altogether, then vitamin B_{12} supplementation is a must. This can be accomplished by eating vitamin B_{12}-fortified foods a few times a day, but a more reliable way is to take a vitamin B_{12} supplement. Talk to your doctor to determine the best dosage for you.

Other nutrients to be mindful of, and great plant-based sources for each, include:

- **Omega-3 fats:** ground flaxseed, chia seeds, hemp seeds, walnuts, algae-based supplements

- **Calcium:** beans and greens (such as pinto and navy beans and broccoli and kale), fortified non-dairy milks

- **Iron:** whole grains, nuts and seeds, fortified breads and cereals (combine with vitamin C–rich foods to increase iron absorption)

- **Iodine:** Iodized salt and seaweed (be mindful of your salt intake due to its blood pressure-elevating effects)

Taking care to eat enough of these foods on a regular basis can ensure that you meet your nutritional requirements. However, everyone is different and individual absorption may vary. It's important to talk to your doctor and consider having bloodwork done to assess your need for any supplementation.

Q: What about protein?

A: Protein deficiency is largely a non-issue, as long as you eat enough calories. In fact, vegetarians and vegans eat only 3 to 4 fewer grams of protein per day than meat eaters do. What's more, in a 2018 study of more than 81,000 adults, eating large amounts of animal protein was shown to increase cardiovascular disease risk by 60%, while large amounts of protein from sources like nuts and seeds decreased that risk by 40%.

Great plant-based sources of protein include:

- Beans and lentils

- Nuts and seeds

- Quinoa

- Oats

- Soy foods such as edamame, tofu, and tempeh

- Sprouted whole-grain bread

Q: Do calories and macros matter?

A: Because this is not a "diet," there are no strict rules. A plant-based lifestyle doesn't include calorie counting or restricting portions (unless you are trying to lose weight, but even then eating an abundance of naturally low-calorie foods often does the trick). Simply listen to your body, eat when you're hungry, and stop when you are comfortably full.

If you still don't see the results you want, the most effective change you can make might be reducing oil consumption. While some studies show the heart-health benefits of extra-virgin olive oil, people who have the most success in reversing heart disease limit or eliminate all added oils from their diet. This has been shown to be a very effective way to improve cholesterol levels, blood pressure, and blood sugar levels.

Q: Can I still have coffee and alcohol?

A: Coffee is high in antioxidants, which may explain its health benefits. In fact, one study showed that moderate coffee consumption (one to three cups daily) is associated with a lower risk of coronary artery disease in women. Another recent study published in the journal *Circulation: Heart Failure* showed a

reduced risk of heart failure in coffee drinkers.

Just be aware of how your body responds to caffeine. Heart palpitations, anxiety, and insomnia may indicate that you are caffeine sensitive and should switch to decaf. Caffeine may also affect blood sugar, so if high blood sugars are an issue for you and you use a blood sugar meter at home, I recommend testing your blood sugars during and after a cup of coffee to see how caffeine affects you.

As for alcohol, no amount has been consistently shown to be beneficial. While red wine is considered heart-healthy, no studies to date have shown a cause-and-effect link. One study actually showed that red wine improved health only when the alcohol was removed, suggesting that the benefits instead come from antioxidants in the grapes.

If you currently drink, the American Heart Association recommends limiting daily consumption to one drink per day for women and two drinks per day for men. And if you don't drink, there's no reason to start.

Overall, water is the drink of choice. Feel free to experiment with flavoring your water by adding fresh lemon or lime juice, mint leaves, berries, or cucumber slices. Other healthy beverage options are unsweetened plant-based milks, green and herbal teas, and decaf coffee.

Q: This is very new to me. What if I can't do it?

A: Successful and long-lasting lifestyle change is about relying on the right tools, following a plan, and incorporating techniques that make habits stick. And that's what this book is all about. We provide you with everything you need to adopt a healthier way of eating for good.

Over the years I've seen hundreds of people make these dietary changes. As a result I've witnessed incredible improvements in health, from dropping triglycerides by 1,000 points (that's not a typo!) to avoiding open-heart surgery. While I can't guarantee you will see the same results—or that it will always be an easy ride—I know you can make significant improvements in your health.

Note that if you decide you are ready for big changes, such as switching from a diet heavy in meat and processed foods to one low in or free of those foods, always talk to your doctor. If you are on blood pressure or diabetes medication (especially insulin), the effect of your medication and these dietary changes will be additive. That is, both your medication and the diet work to lower blood pressure or blood sugars, and there's a chance these effects could combine and result in blood pressure or blood sugars that are too low. Your healthcare provider can advise on any potential need for medication adjustments.

Antioxidants

Shots

Syrup

How to Transition to a Heart-Healthy Diet

The best way to eat to support heart health is to find what is most realistic and sustainable for you. Many people have changed their diet dramatically overnight and have experienced incredible results, fast. Others are more likely to make healthful habits stick when they make gradual changes. Either way, studies clearly show that every step in the direction of a more plant-forward diet can improve your health. So move at a pace that works best for you.

Before we get into food, one initial step must be taken: Ramp up your internal motivation. Take a moment to think about and write down answers to the following questions:

- Why do you want to eat healthier?

- What health improvements do you want to gain? Be specific. For instance, say you want to improve your heart health and energy level. Specific goals could be to lower LDL cholesterol by 10 points and increase average weekday energy level from a 3/10 to an 8/10.

- Describe what your life would look like at your ideal level of health. How do you look and feel? What do you do in your free time? What possibilities does this present for you?

Knowing your "why" can help you stick to your plan when you're struggling, so refer back to your answers any time you need a boost.

Before You Start...

Go through this checklist to set yourself up for success right off the bat.

☐ **Restock your kitchen.**
As they say, if it's in your house, it's in your mouth. So take a look at your fridge and pantry and swap in healthier alternatives for your current foods. Trade white flour for oat or almond flour, use coconut aminos in place of soy sauce, and snack on roasted chickpeas instead of potato chips. Don't remove anything without having a replacement. Check out page 39 for more healthy food swap ideas.

☐ **Stock up on helpful and time-saving cooking tools.**
Many can be bought for less than $5. See "Tools of the Trade" (page 33) for ideas.

☐ **Review your meal plan.**
Each week, look at the plan and your corresponding grocery list, being sure to check your fridge and pantry for ingredients you already have.

☐ **Go food shopping ahead of time.**
Be sure to have everything you need for the week.

☐ **Consider meal or ingredient prepping.**
If you enjoy cooking every day, great! If not, see "Heart-Healthy Meal Prep" (page 37) for tips to make weeknight meals a cinch.

☐ **Keep moving forward.**
Every week, aim to make one or two new small changes in addition to what you're currently doing. Write these down as goals and keep track of how they're going.

Tools of the Trade

You don't need all—or any—of this special equipment to follow this meal plan. However, having some of the below may make cooking and prep work easier and faster.

Storage containers	Silicone baking mat
High-speed or regular blender	Large stockpot
Mini food chopper	Citrus squeezer
Mandoline	Garlic press
Instant Pot	Vegetable peeler
	Potato masher

Don't Stress About Slipups

No matter how much prep work you do, when you're making lifestyle changes, it's normal to fight old habits, deal with cravings, and feel like you should be doing more. Be patient with yourself and your efforts, and know that every slipup is normal, expected, and a chance for you to learn and try it differently the next time.

One unhealthy meal can make a difference, but only in the short term. If your last meal was a heart-unhealthy one, don't sweat it one bit. One week of unhealthy meals, on the other hand, can start to get you into trouble for two main reasons. For one, the health effects can start to become cumulative. And two, it might be harder to bounce back from a week's worth of off-plan meals versus a day's worth.

I recommend planning to be imperfect. But do not have "cheat days." A large, fatty meal can put you at a higher risk of heart attack. In fact, one study found that cardiac deaths are highest on Christmas, followed by the day after Christmas and then New Year's Day, and consuming large amounts of fatty foods is likely the culprit.

If you want to eat foods not on this plan, enjoy them alongside healthier foods. If you must have a burger, have a salad alongside it; or pile lettuce, tomato, and onion on that hoagie. There is evidence that nutrient-rich foods might help offset some of the negative health effects of less-healthful food when eaten together.

And if you do slip up, know that any self-criticism and feelings of failure are much more detrimental to your health than the slipup itself. This is because the event can easily be a one-time thing, but such an emotional response may be enough reason for you to throw your hands in the air and say, "Well it doesn't matter now, I might as well eat whatever I want." Or, worse, it might lead you to give up altogether. Don't beat yourself up. Reassure yourself that eating healthy most of the time can lead to great health.

The Ultimate Heart-Healthy Grocery List

An almost endless array of foods support heart health, and these can be prepared in so many delicious ways. Experiment with new and familiar ingredients and recipes, discovering what you like best. To start, here is a list of foods to consider keeping on hand at all times. It includes many great timesavers and budget-friendly ingredients to make the transition easy on your stress level and your wallet.

VEGETABLES

- ☐ Frozen vegetables * +
- ☐ Dark leafy greens
- ☐ Fresh pre-chopped veggies *
- ☐ Flavor enhancers such as garlic and onion
- ☐ Any other favorites

KEY: * Great time-savers + Budget-friendly

FRUITS

- ☐ Berries
- ☐ Frozen fruit * +
- ☐ Fresh pre-chopped fruit *
- ☐ Dates and other dried fruits
- ☐ Flavor enhancers such as lemons and limes
- ☐ Any other favorites

WHOLE GRAINS

- ☐ Brown rice, quinoa, rolled or steel-cut oats, amaranth, millet, and spelt+
- ☐ Whole-grain or sprouted bread
- ☐ Corn, rice, and wheat tortillas+
- ☐ 10-minute brown rice * +
- ☐ Brown rice noodles+
- ☐ Whole-grain pasta (quinoa, brown rice, chickpeas, whole wheat)+

LEGUMES

- ☐ Dried beans, lentils, peas, and split peas+
- ☐ Canned or frozen legumes (low or no sodium) * +

NUTS & SEEDS

- ☐ Raw, unsalted cashews
- ☐ Ground flaxseed, chia seeds, or hemp seeds
- ☐ Any other favorite raw, unsalted nuts and seeds

BEVERAGES

- [ ] Unsweetened plant milk (almond, cashew, rice, hemp)
- [ ] Green tea
- [ ] Decaf coffee and tea

DIPS, SPREADS, ETC.

- [ ] Salsa
- [ ] Nut and/or seed butters
- [ ] Hummus
- [ ] Tahini
- [ ] Low-sodium hot sauce
- [ ] Mustard (Dijon, yellow, spicy)

PANTRY/FRIDGE

- [ ] Dried herbs, spices, and no-salt blends
- [ ] Canned unsalted tomatoes (crushed, diced, pureed, paste)
- [ ] Vanilla extract
- [ ] Vinegar (balsamic, white or red wine, apple cider, brown rice)
- [ ] Low-sodium vegetable broth
- [ ] Rice crackers or cakes
- [ ] Cacao or cocoa powder
- [ ] Coconut aminos
- [ ] Honey and/or maple syrup
- [ ] Tofu, tempeh, or seitan
- [ ] Whole-grain flours (oat, brown rice, whole wheat, almond, chickpea)
- [ ] Nutritional yeast

Foods to Avoid

While you want to focus on beneficial foods, some foods stand strongly between you and the health you want. If at all possible, it is best to avoid the following foods and seek creative ways to replace them with better alternatives:

- Processed meats such as hot dogs, bacon, ham, pepperoni, and deli meats

- Ultra-processed foods such as soda, potato chips, and sweetened breakfast cereals

- Refined (white) grains such as white bread and instant oatmeal

- High-sodium foods such as frozen meals, salty snacks, pizza, and canned soup (check the labels)

- Fast food

Tips for Eating Out

While on this plan, do not fear social gatherings. There is much to enjoy beyond the food, such as the company, conversation, and connection. These things are truly good for your heart, so savor them!

Your approach to eating out and attending social gatherings will depend on your comfort level and where you are in your health journey. If you don't want to go off track at all because of concerns about your health or that it might derail your efforts, that's OK. Or if you want to sensibly enjoy yourself while out, that's OK too. Do what works for you and use the following tips to make dining away from home a breeze.

AT RESTAURANTS

- Scan the restaurant menu ahead of time. Look for healthier options, and be creative. Think about how existing menu items can be easily modified to better fit your needs.

- Call ahead. Most restaurants are used to various dietary preferences these days. Pick up the phone and find out if they can accommodate your needs and to what extent.

- Seek out ethnic cuisines known for centering their meals more around plants and less around animal-based ingredients.

These include Thai, Chinese, Japanese, Indian, Indonesian, and Ethiopian restaurants.

- Modify Mexican and Italian dishes to better suit your needs. Many can easily be made without high-fat ingredients. If you end up at a steakhouse, check out the salad selections.

- Research your area for healthy local options. Try happycow. net or the Happy Cow app, which lists vegan restaurants in your area. Vegan does not automatically mean they're healthy, but they will provide meat- and dairy-free options to explore.

Heart-Healthy Meal Prep

Meal prep is more than just a trend fueling colorful social media photos. With planning and practice, you can perfect a weekly routine that makes weeknights easier and consistently healthful—and that saves you money, stress, and, ultimately, time.

This can be done with batch cooking. This cooking method includes preparing meals or ingredients in large batches, dividing them into equal portions for the week, and freezing any leftovers. This could be done, for example, by grocery shopping on Saturday and cooking on Sunday morning.

Meal prep means cooking a few meals at once and eating them during the week. This could include:

- ☐ Chili
- ☐ Soup
- ☐ Slow cooker or Instant Pot meals
- ☐ Overnight oats
- ☐ Plant-based muffins
- ☐ Granola bars

Ingredient prep means cooking or preparing a bunch of ingredients at once and using them in various recipes or thrown-together meals. This could include:

- ☐ Chopping or grating veggies or fruit to snack on with a dip or add to salads, oatmeal, or smoothies

- ■ Pick the meeting place. Know of a spot with healthy options? Suggest going there.

- ■ Start with a healthy salad or soup, as well as a glass of water. This will help prevent you from overeating.

- ■ Relax and enjoy. By no means do you need to eat perfectly all of the time. Your overall eating pattern matters most. Enjoy the company and, if need be, balance out a hard-to-resist food with something healthy on the side.

AT PARTIES

- ■ Bring a healthy dish (or two).

- Prepare something you love so others can also enjoy it.

- ■ Call the host ahead of time. Explain your situation, framing the conversation around your health. But don't expect anyone to understand or cook differently. This is simply to ease your mind and let them know you may not eat much or at all.

- ■ Eat beforehand. Have at least a little something healthy before you go. This way you'll be less likely to eat too much of the foods that don't support your heart. You'll also be less tempted to overeat in general.

- ☐ Blanching or steaming veggies

- ☐ Baking potatoes or squash

- ☐ Roasting a batch of veggies for wraps or to put over a grain

- ☐ Cooking a batch of grains, beans, and/or lentils

- ☐ Making sauces or salad dressings

Whether you use one or both methods, a few things can help you get the most from your prep work:

- ■ Create a system, such as themed nights (Taco Tuesday, Pasta Wednesday), or doubling recipes so dinner leftovers can be the next day's lunch.

- ■ Plan out the meals you're going to eat for the week as well as how you'll use repeat ingredients. For example, quinoa can go into Monday's salad, Tuesday's soup, and Thursday's savory breakfast bowl, and the black beans will go in the soup, burgers for Wednesday night, and a dip to snack on with veggies.

- ■ Start with the slowest-cooking ingredients first (usually baked potatoes or whole grains).

- ■ Prep for meal prep! Soak beans overnight and cashews at the start of a cooking session so both are ready to go.

- ■ Stick with versatile breakfasts that are easy and can be made once for multiple mornings, such as overnight oats and chia pudding.

- ■ Visualize your plate when planning meals and snacks. Follow this guide and fill your plate:

½
with vegetables and fruit

¼
with plant-based protein

¼
with whole grains

Eat Right for the Long Haul

This plan isn't about 28 days; it's about making a lifestyle change. So as you go through the next four weeks, keep the following in mind to help you build upon your small accomplishments and continue on the lifelong path toward optimal heart health.

- ■ **Build an arsenal of favorite recipes.** These will be your new go-to meals, the ones you cook so frequently that you no longer need the recipe.

- ■ **Don't sweat it if you don't like something.** This is a time to learn, experiment, and try new things. The more open-minded you are and the more new foods and meals you try, the more healthy options you'll have to rely on in the future.

- ■ **Experiment with different meal-prep methods.** Consider cooking multiple meals ahead of time one or two days a week. The following week, prep multiple ingredients ahead of time. See which method works better for you.

- ■ **Think big picture.** After these 28 days, how will you set yourself up for success? Will you plan a menu each week? Batch cook on Sundays? Cook enough to have leftovers to save you time later in the week? Plan out what a successful week will look like for you.

Heart-Healthy Food Swaps

Certain foods are much better than others for your heart and still satisfy any cravings. Try these replacements.

FOOD	REPLACEMENTS
Butter	Avocado, hummus, or plant-based butter
Milk	Unsweetened non-dairy milk, like almond or soy
Cheese	Nutritional yeast
Beef, sausage, chicken, or turkey	Tofu, tempeh, seitan, or mushroom walnut "ground beef"
Meatballs	Chickpea meatballs or black bean and quinoa meatballs
Buffalo chicken wings	Buffalo cauliflower "wings"
Pulled pork or chicken	Shredded jackfruit
Burgers	Black bean, chickpea, or mushroom burgers
Coconut or palm oil	Flaxseed oil, extra-virgin olive oil, or water sauté when cooking
Scrambled eggs	Tofu scramble
Crackers, popcorn, pretzels, and chips	Homemade oil-free popcorn seasoned with hot sauce or nutritional yeast, crunchy veggies like carrot sticks or snap peas, brown rice crisps or cakes

No-Sodium Flavor Boosters

Rather than reaching for the salt shaker, stock your pantry with these beneficial meal enhancers.

- Salt-free seasoning blends, such as Mrs. Dash or Lawry's Salt Free 17 Seasoning
- Nutritional yeast
- Herbs such as basil, lemongrass, rosemary, oregano, or parsley
- Spices such as paprika, garlic or onion powder, cumin, or coriander
- Sautéed onion and garlic
- Vinegars such as balsamic, apple cider, or red wine
- Coconut aminos
- Lemon, lime, or orange juice and zest
- Raw, cooked, or dried mushrooms
- Low- or no-sodium hot sauce

HOW TO USE THIS BOOK

This 28-day plan is designed to set you up for success. I know it can be hard to make a lot of changes, especially all at once, but I've discovered a few secrets to making it very doable. In addition to the actual eating guide, this program provides three built-in keys to success.

■ **Motivation:** When you consistently eat healthy meals, you're more likely to see results more quickly, whether it be in your cholesterol levels, weight, or energy level. This keeps motivation high during the critical early phase of change when doubt can set in more easily.

■ **Variety and experimentation:** This is a learning opportunity. You'll try new foods, meals, and cooking techniques that you may not have otherwise. This opens doors to more possibilities for healthy eating down the road.

■ **Neuroplasticity:** This is when your taste buds adapt over time to a new way of eating, such as to lower-sodium or lower-fat foods. You not only learn to tolerate these foods but actually love and prefer them.

Now let's talk about the food!
Every meal aligns with what the best available scientific evidence tells us represents a heart-healthy diet: a whole foods, predominantly plant-based menu. This includes foods that are:

- **High fiber.** This powerful cholesterol-lowering nutrient is found only in plants and also increases satiety and supports gut health. Plus, by eating plenty of unprocessed or minimally processed high-fiber foods, you're providing your body with a flood of disease-fighting nutrients and phytochemicals.

- **Low total fat.** Populations with the lowest rates of heart disease obtain about 20% or less of their calories from fat.

- **Low saturated fat,** with the goal of less than 13 grams per day. Saturated fat raises cholesterol levels and can contribute to high blood pressure.

- **Low dietary cholesterol.** Our bodies don't absorb as much from foods as we once thought, but the amount we do absorb can increase blood cholesterol levels. Aim to limit your intake as much as possible.

- **Low sodium,** with a daily goal of less than 1,500 mg. Limiting sodium has been shown to reduce fluid retention in the body, which can lower blood pressure.

Savor the Flavor

Don't let this list trick you: The recipes you're about to try are loaded with satisfying flavor. Many of the foods we eat are drenched in salt, sugar, and added fats. Eating more of a plant-based diet means learning to love the taste of the foods underneath all of those additives—real, whole foods. Along the way, many people discover their cravings disappear. You can effectively regain control over what you want to put in your mouth!

This shift in your taste buds will allow you to enjoy the natural sweetness and hydrating nature of fruit and vegetables, the lightness and freshness of vinegars and lemon juice, the satisfaction of comfort foods like baked potatoes and corn, and the intense transformation in flavor after sautéing garlic and onions or roasting veggies.

You'll also enjoy the nuances of various cuisines from Asian to Mexican to Italian. Instead of taking away from the healthfulness of a dish with salt and vegetable oils, you'll add an unparalleled amount of flavor and nutrition with the liberal use of herbs and spices. Each brings a unique flavor to a dish, from spicy cayenne and tangy sumac to zesty ginger and earthy cumin.

Finally, you'll enjoy a lighter and more healthful twist to some of your old favorites. Experience the richness of blended cashews in a creamy sauce, the satisfying crunch of roasted chickpeas, and the oh-so "cheesy" nature of a nutritional yeast-based meal. If your mouth isn't watering yet, it soon will be!

How the Plan Works

Every week you'll have a shopping list of everything you need. For any packaged items, go straight to the nutrition facts label. Aim to buy foods that include short ingredients lists with words you recognize and can pronounce. Also pay attention to the nutrient content of these foods. Choose those that are lower in total fat, saturated fat, and sodium, and higher in fiber.

Each day includes three meals and two snacks. Feel free to skip the snacks or enjoy any of them as a dessert (or eat some of nature's candy—fruit—to satisfy an after-meal sweet tooth).

Many of the recipes make more than one serving. Plan to eat one per meal or snack and save any leftovers as indicated on the meal plan. That said, no two people have the same appetite, physical activity level, and calorie needs. If the meal plan seems too filling, eat until you are comfortably full, and freeze or save the rest for leftovers. On the other hand, if you find yourself hungry, add more fruit or vegetables to your plate, or consider adding some of the relatively higher-calorie whole grains or legumes to keep you satisfied.

Stay on Track

In addition to a grocery list, meal plan, and recipes, each day you will be provided with a wellness tracker that you'll fill in. This will help you keep tabs on that day's meal plan and also give you an opportunity to focus on other important heart health-related choices around hydration, movement, sleep, and mood.

This type of tracking is shown to help people reach their health goals because it increases awareness, which in turn prompts change. When you see in black and white how much, how little, or how inconsistently you drink water, move, and sleep, you become more cognizant of the areas that need more attention. Then you can create goals and actionable steps outlining exactly how you're going to achieve those objectives.

You will track:

1. HYDRATION

Why: Proper hydration is necessary for good sleep, energy, mental clarity, and bowel function. It also makes the heart's job easier. With adequate fluid volume inside your blood vessels, your ticker doesn't have to work as hard and as fast to deliver oxygen to different parts of your body. While individual needs vary based on activity level, the climate you live in, and more, a good goal to aim for is eight 8-ounce glasses a day.

What you'll record

■ How many glasses of water you drink each day

Key things to know:

■ A quick way to determine if you are dehydrated is to look at your urine. If it is pale and clear, you are well hydrated. However, if it is a dark yellow, it's time to drink more H_2O.

■ Heart medications called diuretics or "water pills" can reduce ankle swelling or blood pressure, but they can also dehydrate. Unless your doctor tells you to limit your fluid intake, be sure to drink adequate amounts of water daily.

■ Caffeinated beverages also act as diuretics. That's all the more reason to sip water throughout the day if you're a coffee lover.

■ Blood pressure medication in combination with dehydration can lead to blood pressure that's too low. Symptoms of low blood pressure include lightheadedness, dizziness, confusion, unusual thirst, and fainting.

Drink up!

■ Buy a reusable water bottle and carry it everywhere.

■ Keep a big jug filled in your fridge for cold water that's ready to go.

■ Jazz up your water with fresh mint or basil leaves, a squeeze of fresh lemon or lime, mashed berries, or cucumber slices.

■ Carry your wellness tracker with you at all times. This may be enough to prompt you to drink more.

2. MOVEMENT

Why: Just like food, exercise is also very medicinal, especially as it pertains to the heart. Exercise can improve and even help eliminate almost all risk factors for heart disease. Exercise also strengthens the heart muscle. The stronger and more "fit" the heart is, the lower your chances of developing heart problems.

Formal exercise isn't the only thing that matters, though. How much you move your body throughout the day is also extremely important. For example, a 2014 study by researchers in Australia reported that interrupting long periods of sitting with two minutes of light walking every 20 minutes can lower both systolic and diastolic blood pressure. So don't go to the gym and then sit on the couch for the rest of the day.

What you'll record

- What type of movement or workout you engaged in

- How long you exercised

- At what intensity you exercised

- How you felt during and after

Key things to know

Always consult your physician prior to starting an exercise program.

Listen to your body. Stop right away if you experience any of the following: pain or discomfort in your chest, neck, jaw, upper back, or one or both arms; shortness of breath; nausea/vomiting; lightheadedness; dizziness; or irregular heartbeat. Inform your doctor right away if symptoms resolve with rest. If they do not, call 911.

Muscle fatigue and mild soreness are normal. Pain and discomfort are not. Again, listen to your body.

If you have high blood pressure or high blood sugars, check your levels before and after exercise, at least until you understand how these parameters respond to exertion. It is normal for both your systolic (top number) blood pressure and blood sugars to be lower after an exercise session.

Move more!

- If exercise is new for you or you haven't exercised in awhile, start slow and keep workouts short, gradually adding more time. Doing too much too soon can result not only in pain and fatigue, it can also squash motivation.

- Track your steps with a step counter or fitness app, wearable fitness tracker, or pedometer. Aim to add 250 to 500 more steps every week until you reach an ideal long-term goal of 7,500 steps or more each day.

- Commit to doing more chores and daily tasks manually, whether it be washing the dishes by hand, walking to the mailbox, or taking the stairs instead of the elevator. Remember, every single time you move counts toward better health.

3. SLEEP

Why: As you saw on page 9, sleep plays a central role in the health of your heart. Inadequate rest can elevate blood pressure, blood sugars, and cravings and also contribute to weight gain, irritability, and even risk of dementia. Get your recommended 7 to 8 hours a night, though, and you can enjoy all the anti-inflammatory, antioxidant, and healing health benefits that come with this daily reboot.

What you'll record

- What time you went to bed

- What time you woke up

Key things to know

- Both quantity and quality matter. If you are having a hard time falling asleep or staying asleep, first evaluate your sleep hygiene, the healthy habits that contribute to a good night's sleep. See the next page for tips.

- If you're practicing good sleep hygiene and still have issues, talk to your doctor.

Sleep soundly!

- Avoid food, alcohol, and sodium before bed, and caffeine after 2 p.m.

- Stick with a consistent sleep schedule. Go to sleep and wake up around the same time every day, even on weekends.

- Get outside. Exposure to sunshine during the day lowers daytime melatonin, while a dark environment during the night raises melatonin levels. This hormone plays an important role in promoting sleep.

- Keep your bedroom dark and cool.

- Move. Use up energy during the day so you aren't wired at night.

- Practice stress-management techniques such as meditation and journaling during the day to quiet mental chatter at night.

- Stay hydrated to keep your nightly core temperature regulated (but don't drink too much close to bedtime).

- Avoid screens at least 30 minutes before bedtime. The blue light is especially alerting for the brain.

- Nap if needed, but keep it short (less than 30 minutes) and not too close to bedtime.

- Establish a relaxing bedtime routine.

4. MOOD

Why: We all have days when we wake up on the wrong side of the bed. However, when a poor mood is a result of stress, worry, anxiety, or depression, it's time to take action. Your body and mind are intimately linked. Negative feelings can increase stress hormones, raise heart rate, and elevate blood pressure. Of course, many different factors can be at play when it comes to these emotions. Tracking your mood throughout this program can help you gain some valuable insight as to how your food and water intake, movement, and sleep affect your feelings.

What you'll record

- Your overall mood for that day

■ If your mood is consistently poor even though you're meeting all of your needs (quality sleep, regular social activities, accepting and receiving emotional support, daily movement, healthy diet), talk with your doctor. It is OK to not be OK. It's also OK to seek additional support; that is what professionals like therapists are for.

Feel great!

■ Be aware of and tend to your needs, including:

☐ Basic needs such as food, water, shelter, clothing, and sleep

☐ Strong and supportive relationships

☐ Respect and self-esteem

☐ A sense of purpose in life

☐ Personal safety, security, and good health

■ Stick to the simple things. Sunshine, nature, a time-out from social media, quiet time to yourself, and saying no can make all the difference in the world when it comes to your emotions and coping skills.

■ If you feel your needs aren't being met or you could use some help in meeting your needs, talk to your doctor or a mental health professional.

No time to cook a full-blown meal? Resist grabbing fast food and try one of these speedy ideas instead.

OATMEAL

½ cup rolled oats +

1 cup unsweetened soy milk +

1 Tbsp ground flaxseed +

½ cup frozen berries

CHIA PUDDING

2 Tbsp chia seeds +

½ cup unsweetened non-dairy milk +

1 tsp honey +

½ cup berries

AVOCADO TOAST

1 slice whole-grain toast +

¼ avocado, mashed +

sprinkle red pepper flakes

PB&S

2 slices whole-wheat bread +

1 Tbsp peanut butter +

sliced strawberries

BURRITO

1 cup cooked 10-minute brown rice +

½ cup canned beans +

¼ avocado, chunked +

¼ cup salsa

PASTA

1 cup cooked chickpea pasta +

½ cup low-sodium tomato sauce +

1 cup frozen mixed veggies +

Italian spices to taste

HUMMUS PITA PIZZA

1 whole wheat pita +
2 Tbsp hummus +
quick-cooking veggies
(i.e., spinach, thinly
sliced zucchini)

CHAPTER 4

28-DAY MEAL PLAN

The following pages include everything you need to begin your heart-healthy eating journey. Before you start each week, review the Week-At-A-Glance chart, and look for the ⓘ symbol to identify dishes you can make ahead. Now let's get started!

Meal Prep 🍴

MAKE

- **Overnight Blueberry Oats (p. 60)**

- **1 hard-boiled egg**

- **Honeydew with Cinnamon Yogurt Dip:** Mix 1 cup **unsweetened coconut yogurt** with ½ tsp **cinnamon**. Chop 3 cups **honeydew melon**. Serves 2.

  Divide melon and dip between 2 airtight containers and refrigerate for Day 2 and 3 snacks.

STORE

Place 4 bananas to the side this week. When they turn very ripe, cut them into chunks. Seal chunks from 1 banana in an airtight bag for the Strawberry Banana Ice Cream, and chunks from the other 3 bananas in a separate bag for the Green Berry Smoothie Bowl, and freeze for week 2 prep.

WEEK 1 AT-A-GLANCE

DAY 1

Breakfast	Pumpkin Chocolate-Chip Oatmeal
Snack	Very Berry Bean Smoothie
Lunch	Vegetable Fried Rice
Snack	2 Tbsp Hummus with 1 cup snap peas + (1) 1 hard-boiled egg
Dinner	Tomato and Basil Spaghetti

DAY 2

Breakfast	(1) Overnight Blueberry Oats
Snack	(1) Honeydew with Cinnamon Yogurt Dip
Lunch	Veggie Sandwich + 1 banana
Snack	Yellow Split Pea Dip + 2 medium carrots, cut into sticks
Dinner	Soba Salad with Chicken

DAY 3

Breakfast	Pumpkin Chocolate-Chip Oatmeal
Snack	Apple with 1 Tbsp nut butter
Lunch	(2) Tomato and Basil Spaghetti
Snack	(1) Honeydew with Cinnamon Yogurt Dip
Dinner	Mediterranean Chicken Bowls

DAY 4

Breakfast	(1) Overnight Blueberry Oats
Snack	Apple with 1 Tbsp nut butter
Lunch	(2) Soba Salad with Chicken
Snack	(2) Yellow Split Pea Dip with 1 medium carrot, cut into sticks
Dinner	Sweet and Sticky Tofu

DAY 5

Breakfast	Sweet Potato Toast with Yogurt and Berries
Snack	2 kiwis (chopped) + ½ cup low-fat plain Greek yogurt
Lunch	(2) Sweet and Sticky Tofu
Snack	2 Tbsp Hummus with 1 cup snap peas
Dinner	Butternut Squash and White Bean Soup

DAY 6

Breakfast	(1) Overnight Blueberry Oats
Snack	1 apple + 1 oz low-fat cheese
Lunch	Veggie Sandwich + 1 banana
Snack	(2) Very Berry Bean Smoothie
Dinner	(2) Mediterranean Chicken Bowls

DAY 7

Breakfast	(2) Sweet Potato Toast with Yogurt and Berries
Snack	1 apple + 1 oz low-fat cheese
Lunch	(2) Butternut Squash and White Bean Soup
Snack	2 kiwis, chopped + ½ cup low-fat plain Greek yogurt
Dinner	Spring Green Panzanella (p. 68) + ½ cup low-sodium chickpeas

Key:

(1) Meal Prep

(2) Leftover

WEEK 1
Shopping List

Buy Just What You Need
Below are exact amounts of every ingredient you will need for Week 1.

PRODUCE

- [ ] 3 apples
- [ ] 9 bananas
- [ ] ¾ cup basil
- [ ] 4 cups blueberries
- [ ] 2 bunches baby bok choy
- [ ] 3 oz broccoli
- [ ] ½ large butternut squash
- [ ] 4 oz purple cabbage
- [ ] 5 carrots
- [ ] 1¾ pints cherry tomatoes
- [ ] 1 small red chile
- [ ] 2 Tbsp cilantro
- [ ] 1 Persian cucumber
- [ ] ½ cup dill
- [ ] 5½ cloves garlic
- [ ] 2¾-in. piece of ginger
- [ ] 3 cups mixed greens
- [ ] ⅓ cup mixed fresh herbs
- [ ] 3 cups honeydew melon
- [ ] 4 kiwis
- [ ] 1¾ lemons
- [ ] 2 onions
- [ ] ½ red onion
- [ ] ½ cup parsley
- [ ] 2 leaves romaine lettuce
- [ ] 8 scallions
- [ ] 2 cups snap peas
- [ ] 4 cups baby spinach
- [ ] 1½ cups strawberries
- [ ] 1 large sweet potato
- [ ] 1 tomato
- [ ] 4 sprigs thyme

MEAT & SEAFOOD

- [ ] 1 lb boneless, skinless chicken breasts
- [ ] 1 cup shredded cooked white-meat chicken

REFRIGERATOR & DAIRY

- [ ] 3 cups unsweetened almond milk
- [ ] ½ cup unsweetened cashew yogurt
- [ ] 2 oz low-fat cheese
- [ ] 1 cup unsweetened coconut yogurt
- [ ] 2 eggs
- [ ] Feta, for serving
- [ ] 1 cup low-fat plain Greek yogurt
- [ ] 8 Tbsp hummus
- [ ] 1 cup nonfat milk
- [ ] 1 14-oz package firm tofu, drained
- [ ] Parmesan, for serving

FROZEN

- [ ] 1 cup frozen cauliflower
- [ ] ¾ cup frozen shelled edamame
- [ ] ¼ cup frozen shelled edamame and peas
- [ ] 7½ Tbsp frozen peas

BREAD & BAKERY

- [ ] 2 thick slices bread
- [ ] 4 slices whole-grain bread

PANTRY

- [ ] 4 Tbsp almond butter
- [ ] 3 dried apricots

- [ ] 1 bay leaf
- [ ] ½ cup brown rice
- [ ] 2 tsp brown sugar
- [ ] 3½ Tbsp canola oil
- [ ] 3 cups low-sodium chicken broth
- [ ] 2½ cups low-sodium canned chickpeas
- [ ] 2 Tbsp mini chocolate chips
- [ ] 4⅛ tsp cinnamon
- [ ] 1 tsp cornstarch
- [ ] 1¼ cups couscous
- [ ] ⅔ tsp Dijon mustard
- [ ] 1 tsp honey
- [ ] ¾ tsp maple syrup
- [ ] 2½ cups rolled oats
- [ ] 5¾ Tbsp olive oil
- [ ] 3 tsp dried oregano
- [ ] 1 cup cooked rice
- [ ] Paprika, for topping
- [ ] 2 Tbsp roasted pistachios
- [ ] ½ cup pumpkin puree
- [ ] 2 Tbsp rice vinegar
- [ ] 4 oz dry soba noodles
- [ ] 3½ Tbsp low-sodium soy sauce
- [ ] 6 oz spaghetti
- [ ] ¼ cup yellow split peas
- [ ] 1 tsp ground sumac
- [ ] 1/16 tsp ground turmeric
- [ ] 4 oz udon noodles
- [ ] 2 cups canned white/cannellini beans
- [ ] ¼ cup dry white wine
- [ ] 2 tsp white wine vinegar
- [ ] 1 tsp vanilla extract

DAY 1: MEAL PLAN

Breakfast	Pumpkin Chocolate-Chip Oatmeal: Cook ½ cup **rolled oats** in ½ cup **nonfat milk** and ½ cup **water**. Stir in ¼ cup **pumpkin puree**, ¼ tsp **cinnamon**, 1 tsp **maple syrup**, and 1 Tbsp **mini chocolate chips**.
Snack	Very Berry Bean Smoothie (p. 60) Freeze remaining in airtight container for Day 6 snack.
Lunch	Vegetable Fried Rice (p. 61)
Snack	2 Tbsp Hummus with 1 cup Snap Peas + 1 Hard-Boiled Egg
Dinner	Tomato and Basil Spaghetti (p. 62) Refrigerate remaining in airtight container for Day 2 lunch.

WATER INTAKE

MOVEMENT/WORKOUT

☐ Yes ☐ No

Activity: _____

_____

Duration: _____

Intensity: _____

SLEEP

Bedtime Last Night: _____

Wake Time This Morning: _____

Mood: 😟 😕 🤪 😐 😃

DAILY NUTRITION: 1,629 cal, 62 g pro, 253 g carb, 36 g fiber, 42 g fat (12.5 g sat fat), 328 mg chol, 1,491 mg sodium

DAY 2: MEAL PLAN

Breakfast	ⓘ Overnight Blueberry Oats (p. 60)
Snack	ⓘ Honeydew with Cinnamon Yogurt Dip
Lunch	Veggie Sandwich + 1 banana Stack 1 leaf **romaine lettuce**, ½ **tomato**, 1 Tbsp **sliced onion**, and ½ **carrot**, shredded, and 2 Tbsp **hummus** between 2 slices of **whole-grain bread**.
Snack	Yellow Split Pea Dip (p. 63) + 2 medium carrots, cut into sticks. Refrigerate remaining dip and 1 sliced carrot in airtight container for Day 4 snack.
Dinner	Soba Salad with Chicken (p. 67) Refrigerate remaining in airtight container for Day 4 lunch.

WATER INTAKE

MOVEMENT/WORKOUT

☐ Yes ☐ No

Activity: _____

_____

Duration: _____

Intensity: _____

SLEEP

Bedtime Last Night: _____

Wake Time This Morning: _____

Mood: 😌 😣 😵 😐 😄

DAILY NUTRITION: 1,462 cal, 70 g pro, 237 g carb, 52 g fiber, 30.5 g fat (7.5 g sat fat), 60 mg chol, 1,163 mg sodium

DAY 3: MEAL PLAN

Breakfast	Pumpkin Chocolate-Chip Oatmeal: Cook ½ cup **rolled oats** in ½ cup **nonfat milk** and ½ cup **water**. Stir in ¼ cup **pumpkin puree**, ¼ tsp **cinnamon**, 1 tsp **maple syrup**, and 1 Tbsp **mini chocolate chips.**
Snack	Apple with 1 Tbsp nut butter
Lunch	♺ Tomato and Basil Spaghetti
Snack	🍴 Honeydew with Cinnamon Yogurt Dip
Dinner	Mediterranean Chicken Bowls (p. 71) Refrigerate remaining in airtight container for Day 6 dinner.

WATER INTAKE

MOVEMENT/WORKOUT

☐ Yes ☐ No

Activity: _____

_____

Duration: _____

Intensity: _____

SLEEP

Bedtime Last Night: _____

Wake Time This Morning: _____

Mood: 😁

DAILY NUTRITION: 1,820 cal, 96 g pro, 271 g carb, 29 g fiber, 43.5 g fat (15 g sat fat), 169 mg chol, 1,238 mg sodium

DAY 4: MEAL PLAN

Breakfast	🍽 Overnight Blueberry Oats
Snack	Apple with 1 Tbsp nut butter
Lunch	♺ Soba Salad with Chicken
Snack	♺ Yellow Split Pea Dip with 1 medium carrot, cut into sticks
Dinner	Sweet and Sticky Tofu (p. 64) Refrigerate remaining in airtight container for Day 5 lunch.

WATER INTAKE

MOVEMENT/WORKOUT

☐ Yes ☐ No

Activity: _____

_____

Duration: _____

Intensity: _____

SLEEP

Bedtime Last Night: _____

Wake Time This Morning: _____

Mood: 😔 😣 🤧 😐 😁

DAILY NUTRITION: 1,354 cal, 72 g pro, 191 g carb, 46 g fiber, 38.5 g fat (5.5 g sat fat), 60 mg chol, 1,014 mg sodium

DAY 5: MEAL PLAN

Breakfast	Sweet Potato Toast with Yogurt and Berries: Preheat oven to 350°F. Slice 1 large **sweet potato** into ¼-in.-thick slices. Place slices in a single layer on lined baking sheet. Bake for 15 to 20 min. until fork-tender but firm enough to hold toppings. Mix ½ cup **unsweetened cashew yogurt**, ½ cup **blueberries**, 2 Tbsp **almond butter**, and ⅛ tsp **cinnamon**. Top half of potatoes with half of yogurt mixture. Serves 2. Refrigerate remaining in airtight container for Day 7 breakfast.
Snack	2 kiwis, chopped + ½ cup low-fat plain Greek yogurt
Lunch	♻ Sweet and Sticky Tofu
Snack	2 Tbsp Hummus with 1 cup Snap Peas
Dinner	Butternut Squash and White Bean Soup (p. 71) Refrigerate remaining in airtight container for Day 7 lunch.

WATER INTAKE

MOVEMENT/WORKOUT

☐ Yes ☐ No

Activity: _____

_____

Duration: _____

Intensity: _____

SLEEP

Bedtime Last Night: _____

Wake Time This Morning: _____

Mood: 😴 😒 🤪 😐 😁

DAILY NUTRITION: 1,315 cal, 62 g pro, 170 g carb, 36 g fiber, 49.5 g fat (7.5 g sat fat), 17 mg chol, 1,037 mg sodium

DAY 6: MEAL PLAN

Breakfast	🍮 Overnight Blueberry Oats
Snack	1 apple + 1 oz low-fat cheese
Lunch	Veggie Sandwich + 1 banana Stack 1 leaf **romaine lettuce**, ½ **tomato**, 1 Tbsp sliced **onion**, and ½ **carrot**, shredded, and 2 Tbsp **hummus** between 2 slices of **whole-grain bread**.
Snack	🔄 Very Berry Bean Smoothie Remove from freezer first thing in the morning to thaw.
Dinner	🔄 Mediterranean Chicken Bowls

WATER INTAKE

MOVEMENT/WORKOUT

☐ Yes   ☐ No

Activity: _____

_____

Duration: _____

Intensity: _____

SLEEP

Bedtime Last Night: _____

Wake Time This Morning: _____

Mood: 😴 😒 🤧 😐 😁

DAILY NUTRITION: 1,853 cal, 107 g pro, 292 g carb, 49 g fiber, 32.5 g fat (7.5 g sat fat), 44 mg chol, 1,558 mg sodium

DAY 7: MEAL PLAN

Breakfast	↻ Sweet Potato Toast with Yogurt and Berries
Snack	1 apple + 1 oz low-fat cheese
Lunch	↻ Butternut Squash and White Bean Soup
Snack	2 kiwis, chopped + ½ cup low-fat plain Greek yogurt
Dinner	Spring Green Panzanella (p. 68) + ½ cup low-sodium chickpeas. Refrigerate remaining panzanella for Day 8 lunch.

WATER INTAKE

MOVEMENT/WORKOUT

☐ Yes ☐ No

Activity: _____

_____

Duration: _____

Intensity: _____

SLEEP

Bedtime Last Night: _____

Wake Time This Morning: _____

Mood: 😔 😣 🤧 😑 😃

DAILY NUTRITION: 1,523 cal, 65 g pro, 209 g carb, 40 g fiber, 55 g fat (10 g sat fat), 27 mg chol, 1,335 mg sodium

Meal Prep

MAKE

- **Chocolate Hummus with Strawberries:** Blend 1 cup low-sodium **chickpeas**, drained and rinsed, 2 Tbsp each **cocoa powder** and **maple syrup**, ⅓ cup **unsweetened almond milk**, and ½ tsp **vanilla extract** until smooth. Serves 2.

  Refrigerate in two airtight containers along with 1 cup strawberries each for Day 8 and 10 snacks.

- **Green Berry Smoothie Bowl:** Blend 3 **frozen bananas**, 3 cups **baby spinach**, 3 cups **frozen strawberries**, ¾ cup **low-sodium cannellini beans**, and 2¼ cups **unsweetened almond milk** until smooth. Divide into two containers and top each with ½ cup **blueberries** and 2 Tbsp **ground flaxseed**. Serves 3.

  Refrigerate one container for Day 8 breakfast and freeze two other containers for Day 13 and Day 15 breakfast.

- **1 hard-boiled egg**

STORE

Place 1 **banana** to the side this week. When it turns very ripe, cut it into chunks, seal in an airtight bag, and freeze for the Banana Bread Smoothie.

Very Berry Bean Smoothie

Cannellini beans are a great source of heart-healthy fiber. They add extra creaminess to this smoothie, but you won't taste them—the fruit and vanilla completely mask the flavor!

ACTIVE 5 MIN. | TOTAL 5 MIN. | SERVES 2

1 cup strawberries
1 cup blueberries
1 cup frozen cauliflower
1 banana
½ cup canned low-sodium cannellini beans (drained and rinsed)
1 tsp vanilla extract

Directions: Blend all ingredients plus ½ cup water until smooth.

Tip: Freeze remaining smoothie in airtight container for Day 6 snack.

PER SERVING: 256 cal, 9 g pro, 54 g carb, 13 g fiber, 21 g sugars (0 g added sugars), 1 g fat (0 g sat fat), 0 g chol, 20 mg sodium

Overnight Blueberry Oats

It's easy to eat right when you have something delicious waiting for you in the fridge. Prepare this recipe the night before Day 2 for a hearty breakfast you can enjoy all week.

ACTIVE 10 MIN. | TOTAL 10 MIN. (plus 8 hr. in fridge) SERVES 3

1½ cups rolled oats
3 cups unsweetened almond milk
3 cups blueberries
3 tsp cinnamon
1 tsp vanilla extract

Directions: Combine all ingredients in airtight container. Place in fridge overnight.

PER SERVING: 303 cal, 9 g pro, 51 g carb, 12 g fiber, 16 g sugars (0 g added sugars), 6 g fat (1 g sat), 0 mg chol, 165 mg sodium

Vegetable Fried Rice

Broccoli is the heart-healthy superstar in this dish. It's packed with anti-inflammatory phytonutrients and blood vessel-healing potassium, folate, and vitamin C.

ACTIVE 15 MIN. | TOTAL 15 MIN. | SERVES 4

12 oz chopped broccoli
2 scallions (white part only), finely chopped, plus more for garnish
2 cloves garlic, finely chopped
1 1-in. piece peeled ginger, finely chopped
2 Tbsp olive oil, divided
4 cups cooked rice
3 eggs
1 cup frozen shelled edamame and peas (thawed)
3 Tbsp low-sodium soy sauce
1 Tbsp honey
1 Tbsp rice vinegar

Directions: In a large nonstick skillet, cook broccoli in 3 Tbsp water, covered, for 2 min. Add scallions, garlic, and ginger; stir-fry for 1 minute. Add 1 Tbsp oil and rice; cook, and toss until rice starts to crisp.

Push rice to one side of skillet, add 1 Tbsp oil to empty side; scramble eggs. Fold into rice with edamame and peas, soy sauce, honey, and vinegar. Top with 2 scallions (white part only), finely chopped, plus more for garnish.

PER SERVING: 434 cal, 18 g pro, 63 g carb, 7 g fiber, 8 g sugars (4 g added sugars), 13 g fat (2 g sat fat), 139 mg chol, 765 mg sodium

Tomato and Basil Spaghetti

This dish's authentic Italian flavor is thanks to fresh parsley and basil, two herbs rich in vitamin K, a nutrient known to decrease risk of coronary heart disease.

ACTIVE 20 MIN. | TOTAL 20 MIN. | SERVES 2

6 oz spaghetti
1 clove garlic, thinly sliced
½ small red onion, thinly sliced
1 lemon, 2 strips zest removed and thinly sliced, plus 1 Tbsp lemon juice
¼ cup dry white wine
1 Tbsp olive oil
Kosher salt and pepper
1½ cups cherry or grape tomatoes, assorted colors, halved
¼ cup parsley leaves, roughly chopped
½ cup basil leaves, roughly chopped
Grated Parmesan, for serving

Directions: In medium skillet or Dutch oven, place spaghetti (it should lie flat on the bottom). Add garlic, onion, lemon juice, wine, oil, 2 cups water, ½ tsp salt, and ¼ tsp pepper. Bring to a boil and boil gently, stirring frequently, 5 minutes.

Fold in tomatoes and continue to boil gently until pasta is al dente and nearly all liquid has been absorbed (absorption will continue).

Stir in lemon zest and parsley, then fold in basil. Serve with grated Parmesan if desired.

PER SERVING: 430 cal, 14 g pro, 73 g carb, 6 g fiber, 4 g sugars (0 g added sugars), 9 g fat (1.5 g sat), 0 mg chol, 385 mg sodium

Yellow Split Pea Dip

As eye-catching as it is appetizing, this high-fiber dip contains anti-inflammatory turmeric to boost your immune system.

ACTIVE 10 MIN. | TOTAL 1 HR. 10 MIN. SERVES 8

- 1 cup yellow split peas
- 1 small onion, finely chopped
- 1 large clove garlic, pressed
- 1 bay leaf
- ½ tsp ground turmeric
- Kosher salt
- 2 Tbsp olive oil, plus more for topping
- 1 Tbsp fresh lemon juice
- Finely chopped red onion, finely chopped parsley, and paprika, for topping

Directions: In small saucepan, combine split peas with 2½ cups water and bring to boil, skimming foam that rises to surface. Reduce heat and add onion, garlic, bay leaf, turmeric, and ½ tsp salt and simmer until split peas are very tender, 1 hour.

Discard bay leaf and transfer split pea mixture to food processor with any remaining liquid. Add olive oil and lemon juice and puree until smooth.

Serve drizzled with additional olive oil and topped with red onion, parsley, and sprinkle of paprika if desired.

PER SERVING: 130 cal, 6 g pro, 18 g carb, 7 g fiber, 1 g sugars (0 g added sugars), 4.5 g fat (0.5 g sat), 0 mg chol, 120 mg sodium (2 g sat fat), 139 mg chol, 765 mg sodium

Sweet and Sticky Tofu

Made of soy and high in protein, tofu is a plant-based-diet staple. It takes on the flavor of sauces and marinades so there are countless ways to prepare it. This version is perfectly sweet and savory.

ACTIVE 30 MIN. | TOTAL 30 MIN.
SERVES 2

4 oz udon noodles
2 Tbsp low-sodium soy sauce
1 tsp brown sugar
1 tsp cornstarch
Black pepper
1 14-oz package firm tofu, drained
2 Tbsp canola oil, divided
2 cloves garlic, finely chopped
1 1-in. piece fresh ginger, peeled and cut into matchsticks
4 scallions, thinly sliced, divided
1 small red chile, thinly sliced
2 bunches baby bok choy, leaves separated and halved lengthwise
2 cups baby spinach

Directions: Cook udon noodles per pkg. directions. In a small bowl, combine ¼ cup water, soy sauce, brown sugar, cornstarch, and ½ tsp pepper until smooth.

Blot tofu dry with paper towels. Cut into ¾-in. pieces. Heat a large skillet on medium-high. Add 1 Tbsp oil, then tofu, and cook, stirring occasionally, until golden brown, 6 to 8 minutes. Transfer to a plate; wipe out skillet.

Add remaining Tbsp oil, then garlic, ginger, and half the scallions and chile and cook 1 minute. Add bok choy and cook, tossing, 2 minutes.

Fold in tofu, then soy sauce mixture. Simmer until thickened, about 1 minute; toss with spinach. Spoon over cooked udon noodles and top with remaining scallions and chile.

PER SERVING: 270 cal, 15 g pro, 27 g carb, 5 g fiber, 3 g sugars (1 g added sugars), 12 g fat (1 g sat fat), 0 mg cholesterol, 405 mg sodium

Soba Salad with Chicken

Soba noodles are made of buckwheat, a pseudo-grain known for its cholesterol-lowering effects, which come from the antioxidant rutin.

ACTIVE 15 MIN. | TOTAL 15 MIN. | SERVES 2

4 oz dry soba noodles or whole-wheat spaghetti

½ cup frozen shelled edamame

4 oz shredded purple cabbage

1 cup shredded cooked white-meat chicken

1 scallion, thinly sliced

4 oz carrots (cut into ½-in. pieces)

1 Tbsp finely grated fresh ginger

2 Tbsp rice vinegar

½ Tbsp low-sodium soy sauce

1 tsp light brown sugar

2 Tbsp canola oil

Directions: Cook noodles per pkg. directions, adding edamame during the last minute of cooking. Drain; run under cold water to cool.

Toss cabbage with chicken and scallions.

In a mini food processor, finely chop carrots, then add ginger, vinegar, soy sauce, and sugar.

With the processor running, slowly add oil until fully incorporated. Toss 2 Tbsp with noodles, then fold in chicken mixture. Serve with remaining dressing and sprinkle with sesame seeds if desired.

PER SERVING: 408 cal, 37 g pro, 54 g carb, 14 g fiber, 4 g sugars (0 g added sugars), 7 g fat (1 g sat fat), 60 mg chol, 234 mg sodium

Spring Green Panzanella

There may be bread in this recipe, but with scallions, peas, fresh herbs, plus greens tossed in a bright vinaigrette, this totally counts as a salad.

ACTIVE 20 MIN. | TOTAL 20 MIN. | SERVES 2

2 thick slices bread (about 4 oz, preferably stale)
2½ Tbsp olive oil, divided
2 tsp white wine vinegar
½ tsp Dijon mustard
Kosher salt and pepper
1 scallion, white and light green parts finely chopped, dark green parts thinly sliced
1 Persian cucumber, smashed, halved lengthwise and then sliced
¼ cup fresh or frozen peas (thawed if frozen)
¾ cups mixed fresh herbs (such as parsley, basil, mint, and dill)
3 cups mixed greens

Directions: Heat oven to 400°F. Cut crusts off bread and tear bread into large pieces. On rimmed baking sheet, toss bread with 1 Tbsp oil and roast until golden brown, about 10 minutes.

Meanwhile, in a large bowl, whisk together vinegar, mustard, remaining 1½ Tbsp oil, and pinch each salt and pepper; stir in chopped scallions.

Add cucumber and toss to coat, then toss with toasted bread. Add peas, herbs, and greens and toss gently to combine.

PER SERVING: 315 cal, 7 g pro, 32 g carb, 5 g fiber, 3 g sugars (0 g added sugars), 18.5 g fat (2.5 g sat fat), 0 mg chol, 480 mg sodium

Butternut Squash and White Bean Soup

Looking to lower your blood pressure? Look no further! Both the butternut squash and the white beans in this recipe pack a big punch of potassium, an important blood pressure-lowering nutrient.

ACTIVE 25 MIN. | TOTAL 45 MIN. | SERVES 2

1½ Tbsp olive oil
½ onion, chopped
½ large butternut squash, neck only, peeled and cut into ½-in. pieces
2 cloves garlic, finely chopped
½ Tbsp finely chopped peeled fresh ginger
3 cups low-sodium chicken broth
4 sprigs fresh thyme
½ 15-oz can white beans, rinsed
½ 15-oz can chickpeas, rinsed
¼ cup couscous
2 Tbsp roasted pistachios, finely chopped
2 Tbsp cilantro, roughly chopped
3 dried apricots, finely chopped
1 scallion, thinly sliced

Directions: Heat oil in a Dutch oven on medium. Add onion and cook, covered, stirring occasionally, 6 minutes. Add squash and cook, covered, stirring occasionally for 8 minutes. Stir in garlic and ginger and cook 1 minute. Add broth and thyme and bring to a boil.

Using a fork, mash white beans and add to soup along with chickpeas.

Cook couscous per pkg. directions; fluff with a fork and fold in pistachios, cilantro, apricots, and scallion. Serve soup topped with couscous mixture.

PER SERVING: 565 cal, 25 g pro, 82 g carb, 18 g fiber, 12 g sugars (0 g added sugars), 17.5 g fat (2.5 g sat fat), 0 mg chol, 385 mg sodium

Air-Fryer Mediterranean Chicken Bowls

Cooking the chicken in an air fryer gives it all the crispy flavor of deep-frying but in a heart-healthy way! You only need 1 Tbsp of oil to get a delicious golden hue.

ACTIVE 15 MIN. | TOTAL 30 MIN.
SERVES 2

1 lb boneless, skinless chicken breasts, cut into 1½-in. pieces

1 Tbsp olive oil

1 tsp dried oregano

1 tsp ground sumac

Kosher salt and pepper

1 pint grape or cherry tomatoes

1 medium onion, roughly chopped

1 cup couscous

1 tsp grated lemon zest plus 1 Tbsp lemon juice, plus lemon wedges for serving

4 Tbsp fresh dill, divided

Crumbled feta, for serving

Directions: In large bowl, toss the chicken with the oil, then the oregano, sumac, and ½ tsp each salt and pepper. Add the tomatoes and onion and toss to combine.

Arrange in an even layer in an air-fryer basket and air-fry at 400°F, shaking the basket occasionally, until the chicken is golden brown and cooked through, 15 to 20 minutes.

Meanwhile, in a medium pot, bring 1¼ cups water to a boil. Toss the couscous with the lemon zest and add to the boiling water. Stir, cover, remove from heat, and let stand for 5 minutes. Fluff with a fork and fold in the lemon juice and 2 Tbsp of the dill.

Serve the chicken and vegetables over the couscous, spooning any juices collected at the bottom of the air fryer over the top. Sprinkle with the remaining 2 Tbsp dill and feta and serve with the lemon wedges if desired.

PER SERVING: 718 cal, 65 g pro, 88 g carb, 8 g fiber, 5 g sugars (0 g added sugars), 13.5 g fat (2.4 g sat fat), 166 mg chol, 662 mg sodium

NO AIR FRYER?

Not a problem! Arrange the chicken, seasonings, tomatoes, and onion on a baking sheet and bake at 425°F until the chicken is golden brown and cooked through, 15 to 20 minutes.

WEEK 2 AT-A-GLANCE

DAY 8

Breakfast	🍴 Green Berry Smoothie Bowl
Snack	🍴 Chocolate Hummus with Strawberries
Lunch	♺ Spring Green Panzanella + ½ cup low-sodium chickpeas
Snack	1 sliced pear with 1 Tbsp all-natural peanut butter
Dinner	Salmon with Citrusy Lentil Salad

DAY 9

Breakfast	Skillet Berry French Toast
Snack	1 sliced pear with 1 Tbsp all-natural peanut butter
Lunch	Speedy Black Beans and Rice
Snack	1 cup strawberries + ½ cup low-fat plain Greek yogurt
Dinner	Chickpea Curry + Garlic Ginger Sautéed Spinach

DAY 10

Breakfast	🍴 Mashed Sweet Potato Bowl
Snack	🍴 Chocolate Hummus with Strawberries
Lunch	♺ Salmon with Citrusy Lentil Salad
Snack	1 sliced pear with 1 Tbsp all-natural peanut butter
Dinner	Creamy Vegan Linguine with Wild Mushrooms

DAY 11

Breakfast	♺ Skillet Berry French Toast
Snack	🍴 Smoky Roasted Chickpeas
Lunch	♺ Speedy Black Beans and Rice
Snack	Strawberry Banana Nice Cream
Dinner	♺ Chickpea Curry + ♺ Garlic Ginger Sautéed Spinach

DAY 12

Breakfast	🍴 Mashed Sweet Potato Bowl + 1 hard-boiled egg
Snack	1 sliced pear with 1 Tbsp all-natural peanut butter
Lunch	♺ Creamy Vegan Linguine with Wild Mushrooms
Snack	1 cup strawberries + ½ cup low-fat plain Greek yogurt
Dinner	Tofu Pad Thai

DAY 13

Breakfast	Green Berry Smoothie Bowl
Snack	🍴 Smoky Roasted Chickpeas
Lunch	♺ Speedy Black Beans and Rice
Snack	♺ Strawberry Banana Nice Cream
Dinner	Spiced Cod with Rice Noodle Salad

Key:

🍴 Meal Prep

♺ Leftover

WEEK 2
Shopping List

Buy Just What You Need
Below are exact amounts of every ingredient you will need for Week 2. Check for leftover ingredients from Week 1 before purchasing new ingredients from the list.

PRODUCE
- [ ] ½ small apple
- [ ] 3 cups arugula
- [ ] 6 bananas
- [ ] 4 Tbsp basil
- [ ] 1½ cups blueberries
- [ ] 2 cups broccoli florets
- [ ] Cilantro, for serving
- [ ] ½ red chile, seeded and thinly sliced
- [ ] 1½ Tbsp chives
- [ ] ½ small English cucumber
- [ ] 3½ Tbsp chopped dill
- [ ] 5½ cloves garlic
- [ ] 3½-in. piece ginger
- [ ] 1⅓ green onion
- [ ] ⅓ cup mixed fresh herbs (basil, parsley, dill, chives)
- [ ] 4 kiwis
- [ ] ¾ lemon
- [ ] 2 limes
- [ ] 1 cup mung bean sprouts
- [ ] 4 oz mixed mushrooms
- [ ] ½ onion
- [ ] 1½ Tbsp flat leaf parsley
- [ ] 4 pears
- [ ] 2 small radishes
- [ ] 2 scallions
- [ ] ½ cup snow peas
- [ ] 13 cups spinach
- [ ] 5 cups strawberries
- [ ] 2 sweet potatoes
- [ ] 1 Tbsp tarragon

MEAT & SEAFOOD
- [ ] 8 oz skinless cod fillet
- [ ] 10 oz skinless salmon fillet

REFRIGERATOR & DAIRY
- [ ] 4 cups unsweetened almond milk
- [ ] 5 large eggs
- [ ] ½ cup low-fat milk
- [ ] 1 cup low-fat plain Greek yogurt
- [ ] ¼ cup shaved Parmesan
- [ ] 7 oz extra-firm tofu
- [ ] Yogurt, for serving

FROZEN
- [ ] 4 cups frozen mixed berries
- [ ] 5 cups frozen strawberries

BREAD & BAKERY
- [ ] 5 slices whole-grain bread

PANTRY
- [ ] 1 15-oz can low-sodium black beans
- [ ] ¾ cup low-sodium cannellini beans
- [ ] 4½ cups low-sodium canned chickpeas
- [ ] 1 tsp chili powder
- [ ] ½ tsp ground cinnamon
- [ ] ½ cup low-sodium chicken broth
- [ ] ½ tsp sweet chili sauce
- [ ] 2 Tbsp cocoa powder
- [ ] ½ cup light coconut milk
- [ ] 1½ Tbsp cornstarch
- [ ] Confectioners' sugar for serving
- [ ] 2½ tsp cumin
- [ ] ½ Tbsp curry powder
- [ ] ½ Tbsp fish sauce
- [ ] 10 Tbsp ground flaxseed
- [ ] ⅛ tsp garlic powder
- [ ] ½ 15-oz can lentils
- [ ] 6 oz linguine or fettuccine
- [ ] 2½ Tbsp maple syrup
- [ ] ⅛ tsp ground nutmeg
- [ ] 4 oz rice vermicelli noodles
- [ ] 3 Tbsp nutritional yeast
- [ ] 7 Tbsp olive oil
- [ ] 2 Tbsp oil
- [ ] 1 tsp onion powder
- [ ] 1 tsp oregano
- [ ] 1 Tbsp smoked paprika
- [ ] 4 oz short pasta (like rotini)
- [ ] 3 Tbsp chopped peanuts
- [ ] 6⅓ Tbsp all-natural peanut butter
- [ ] 2 Tbsp golden raisins
- [ ] ¼ tsp crushed red pepper flakes
- [ ] 1 cup 10-minute brown rice
- [ ] ½ cup long-grain white rice
- [ ] 2 Tbsp low-sodium soy sauce
- [ ] 1 tsp sugar
- [ ] 1 15-oz can fire-roasted tomatoes
- [ ] ¼ tsp ground turmeric
- [ ] 1 Tbsp red wine vinegar
- [ ] 1 tsp pure vanilla extract

DAY 8: MEAL PLAN

Breakfast	(i) Green Berry Smoothie Bowl
Snack	(i) Chocolate Hummus with Strawberries
Lunch	(c) Spring Green Panzanella + ½ cup low-sodium chickpeas
Snack	1 sliced pear with 1 Tbsp all-natural peanut butter
Dinner	Salmon with Citrusy Lentil Salad (p. 82) Refrigerate remaining in airtight container for Day 10 lunch.

WATER INTAKE

MOVEMENT/WORKOUT

☐ Yes ☐ No

Activity: _____

_____

Duration: _____

Intensity: _____

SLEEP

Bedtime Last Night: _____

Wake Time This Morning: _____

Mood: 😔 😒 🤧 😑 😄

DAILY NUTRITION: 1,591 cal, 73 g pro, 230 g carb, 54 g fiber, 51 g fat (7.5 g sat fat), 66 mg chol, 1,087 mg sodium

DAY 9: MEAL PLAN

Breakfast	Skillet Berry French Toast (p. 84)
Snack	1 sliced pear with 1 Tbsp peanut butter
Lunch	Speedy Black Beans and Rice: Cook 1 cup **10-minute brown rice** per pkg. directions. In pan over medium-low heat, add 1 15-oz can **low-sodium black beans** (drained and rinsed); 1 15-oz can **fire-roasted tomatoes**; 1 tsp each of **cumin**, **oregano**, **chili powder**, and **onion powder;** and ⅛ tsp **garlic powder**. Cover and simmer for 10 minutes, then mix in the rice. Serves 3. Refrigerate remaining in airtight container for Day 10 and Day 13 lunch.
Snack	1 cup strawberries + ½ cup low-fat plain Greek yogurt
Dinner	Chickpea Curry (p. 83) + Garlic Ginger Sautéed Spinach: Heat 1-2 Tbsp **water** in a medium skillet over medium-high heat. Saute 1 lb **spinach**, 2 cloves minced **garlic**, and 1½ tsp grated **ginger** until wilted. **Salt** and **pepper** to taste. Serves 2. Refrigerate remaining in airtight container for Day 11 dinner.

WATER INTAKE

MOVEMENT/WORKOUT

☐ Yes ☐ No

Activity: _____

Duration: _____

Intensity: _____

Meal Prep

MAKE

■ **Mashed Sweet Potato Bowl:** Cut 2 **sweet potatoes** in half and bake, cut side down, at 400°F for 30 minutes or until pierced easily with fork. Let cool. Scoop insides into a bowl, add ¼ cup **unsweetened almond milk**, and mash well with the back of a fork. Mix in ¼ cup **ground flaxseed** and 1 cup **blueberries**. Serves 2.

Refrigerate in airtight container for Day 10 and 13 breakfasts.

SLEEP

Bedtime Last Night: _____

Wake Time This Morning: _____

Mood: 😔 😣 🤢 😐 😁

DAILY NUTRITION: 1,585 cal, 66 g pro, 263 g carb, 42 g fiber, 35 g fat (12 g sat fat), 206 mg chol, 1,063 mg sodium

Meal Prep

MAKE

■ **Smoky Roasted Chickpeas:** Drain and rinse 2¼ cups **low-sodium chickpeas**. Spread out on absorbent towel, cover with second towel, and roll around until very dry. Transfer to bowl and mix with 1 Tbsp **smoked paprika**, 1½ tsp **cumin**, and ⅓ tsp **salt**. Roast at 350°F for 35 to 40 minutes, shaking baking sheet every 10 minutes or so. Let cool. Serves 3.

Cool completely and store in an airtight container at room temperature for Day 11, 13, and 14 snacks. Recrisp in a toaster oven as necessary.

DAY 10: MEAL PLAN

Breakfast	Mashed Sweet Potato Bowl
Snack	Chocolate Hummus with Strawberries
Lunch	Salmon with Citrusy Lentil Salad
Snack	1 sliced pear with 1 Tbsp all-natural peanut butter
Dinner	Creamy Vegan Linguine with Wild Mushrooms (p. 85). Refrigerate remaining in airtight container for Day 12 lunch.

WATER INTAKE

MOVEMENT/WORKOUT

☐ Yes ☐ No

Activity: _____

Duration: _____

Intensity: _____

SLEEP

Bedtime Last Night: _____

Wake Time This Morning: _____

Mood: 😒 😣 😵 😐 😄

DAILY NUTRITION: 1,440 cal, 70 g pro, 206 g carb, 40 g fiber, 42.5 g fat, 7 g sat fat, 66 mg chol, 588 mg sodium

DAY 11: MEAL PLAN

Breakfast	↻ Skillet Berry French Toast
Snack	🍴 Smoky Roasted Chickpeas
Lunch	↻ Speedy Black Beans and Rice
Snack	Strawberry Banana Nice Cream: Blend 2 cups **frozen strawberries**, ½ cup frozen **banana**, and 3½ Tbsp **unsweetened almond milk** until smooth. Serves 2. Freeze remaining in airtight container for Day 13 snack.
Dinner	↻ Chickpea Curry + ↻ Garlic Ginger Sautéed Spinach

WATER INTAKE

MOVEMENT/WORKOUT

☐ Yes ☐ No

Activity: _____

_____

Duration: _____

Intensity: _____

SLEEP

Bedtime Last Night: _____

Wake Time This Morning: _____

Mood: 😣 😠 🤧 😐 😄

DAILY NUTRITION: 1,595 cal, 63 g pro, 283 g carb, 49 g fiber, 29 g fat (8 g sat fat), 189 mg chol, 1,318 mg sodium

DAY 12: MEAL PLAN

Breakfast	Mashed Sweet Potato Bowl + 1 hard-boiled egg
Snack	1 sliced pear with 1 Tbsp all-natural peanut butter
Lunch	Creamy Vegan Linguine with Wild Mushrooms
Snack	1 cup strawberries + ½ cup low-fat plain Greek yogurt
Dinner	Tofu Pad Thai (p. 86) Refrigerate remaining in airtight container for Day 14 lunch.

WATER INTAKE

MOVEMENT/WORKOUT

☐ Yes   ☐ No

Activity: _____

_____

Duration: _____

Intensity: _____

SLEEP

Bedtime Last Night: _____

Wake Time This Morning: _____

Mood: 😴 😒 🤧 😐 😄

DAILY NUTRITION: 1,506 cal, 59 g pro, 224 g carb, 28 g fiber, 46 g fat (9.5 g sat fat), 203 mg chol, 1,035 mg sodium

DAY 13: MEAL PLAN

Breakfast	ⓘ Green Berry Smoothie Bowl
Snack	ⓘ Smoky Roasted Chickpeas
Lunch	⟳ Speedy Black Beans and Rice
Snack	⟳ Strawberry Banana Nice Cream
Dinner	Spiced Cod with Rice Noodle Salad (p. 87) Refrigerate remaining in airtight container for Day 15 lunch.

WATER INTAKE

MOVEMENT/WORKOUT

☐ Yes ☐ No

Activity: _____

_____

Duration: _____

Intensity: _____

SLEEP

Bedtime Last Night: _____

Wake Time This Morning: _____

Mood: 😟 😠 🤪 😐 😁

DAILY NUTRITION: 1,574 cal, 62 g pro, 271 g carb, 49 g fiber, 34 g fat (2.5 g sat fat), 43 mg chol, 1,418 mg sodium

DAY 14: MEAL PLAN

Breakfast	Spicy Veggie Sauté (p. 87) Refrigerate remaining in airtight container for Day 16 breakfast.
Snack	1 banana + 2 tsp all-natural peanut butter
Lunch	♺ Tofu Pad Thai
Snack	Smoky Roasted Chickpeas
Dinner	Lemon-Marinated Herb Pasta Salad (p. 88) + Steamed Broccoli: Steam 2 cups **broccoli florets** for 5 to 7 minutes. Toss with 1½ Tbsp **nutritional yeast**, 1 clove **garlic**, minced, and ½ **lemon**, juiced and zested. **Salt** and **pepper** to taste. Serves 2. Refrigerate remaining in airtight container for Day 16 lunch.

WATER INTAKE

MOVEMENT/WORKOUT

☐ Yes ☐ No

Activity: _____

_____

Duration: _____

Intensity: _____

SLEEP

Bedtime Last Night: _____

Wake Time This Morning: _____

Mood: 😴 😠 🤧 😐 😄

DAILY NUTRITION: 1,622 cal, 67 g pro, 238 g carb, 36 g fiber, 51.5 g fat (10 g sat fat), 199 mg chol, 1,716 mg sodium

Salmon with Citrusy Lentil Salad

This hearty dinner, full of protein-packed lentils and heart-healthy salmon, takes only 15 minutes to cook.

ACTIVE 15 MIN. | TOTAL 15 MIN.
SERVES 2

1 Tbsp olive oil, divided
2 5-oz pieces skinless salmon fillet
Kosher salt and pepper
1 Tbsp red wine vinegar
½ 15-oz can lentils, rinsed
½ small English cucumber, cut into pieces
½ pink grapefruit, peel and pith removed, cut into pieces
2 small radishes, thinly sliced
2 cups arugula

Directions: Heat ½ Tbsp oil in a small nonstick skillet on medium. Season salmon with ¼ tsp each salt and pepper and cook until golden brown, about 7 minutes. Turn salmon over and continue cooking until just opaque throughout, about 2 minutes more.

Meanwhile, in bowl, whisk together vinegar and remaining ½ Tbsp oil. Add lentils and toss to coat then toss with cucumber, grapefruit, and radishes. Fold in arugula and serve with salmon.

PER SERVING: 330 cal, 36 g pro, 22 g carb, 9 g fiber, 3 g sugars (0 g added sugars), 10.5 g fat (2 g sat fat), 66 mg chol, 275 mg sodium

Chickpea Curry

Chickpeas are packed with heart-healthy benefits. They're both high in soluble fiber and low in fat, the perfect combination for lowering cholesterol.

ACTIVE 20 MIN. | TOTAL 20 MIN. | SERVES 2

½ cup long-grain white rice
1 Tbsp olive oil
½ onion, finely chopped
1 clove garlic, finely chopped
1½-in. piece peeled ginger, finely chopped
½ Tbsp curry powder
½ 15-oz can chickpeas, rinsed
½ small apple, chopped
½ cup light coconut milk
½ cup low-sodium chicken broth
2 Tbsp golden raisins
Chopped cilantro, for serving

Directions: Cook rice according to pkg. directions.

Heat oil in a medium skillet on medium. Add onion and sauté for 4 minutes. Stir in garlic and ginger and cook 2 minutes.

Add the curry powder and cook, stirring, for 1 minute. Add chickpeas, apple, coconut milk, chicken broth, and raisins and simmer for 5 minutes. Serve over the rice and top with cilantro, if desired.

PER SERVING: 460 cal, 12 g pro, 75 g carb, 7 g fiber, 15 g sugars (0 g added sugars), 13 g fat (5 g sat fat), 0 mg chol, 170 mg sodium

Skillet Berry French Toast

This breakfast dish is both sweet and heart-healthy, thanks to the mixed berries. Berries have been shown to improve HDL or "good" cholesterol, which is no easy feat.

ACTIVE 10 MIN. | TOTAL 30 MIN. | SERVES 2

- 1 10-oz pkg. frozen mixed berries (about 4 cups)
- ½ Tbsp grated fresh ginger
- ½ Tbsp cornstarch
- 1 tsp finely grated lime zest
- 2 large eggs
- ½ cup low-fat milk
- ½ Tbsp maple syrup
- ½ tsp pure vanilla extract
- ¼ tsp ground cinnamon
- ⅛ tsp ground nutmeg
- 3 slices whole-grain bread
- Confectioners' sugar and yogurt, for serving

Directions: Heat oven to 425°F. In small cast-iron skillet, combine berries, ginger, cornstarch, and lime zest.

In medium bowl, whisk together eggs, milk, maple syrup, vanilla, cinnamon, and nutmeg. Dip bread slices in egg mixture and arrange in a circle, overlapping, on top of berries.

Bake until golden brown, 18 to 20 minutes. Dust with confectioners' sugar and serve with yogurt if desired.

PER SERVING: 355 cal, 17 g pro, 56 g carb, 10 g fiber, 24 g sugars (9 g added sugars), 7 g fat (2 g sat fat), 189 mg chol, 325 mg sodium

Creamy Vegan Linguine with Wild Mushrooms

This recipe proves that you don't need cream for a truly decadent pasta dish.

ACTIVE 20 MIN.
TOTAL 20 MIN.
SERVES 2

6 oz linguine or fettuccine

2 Tbsp olive oil

4 oz mixed mushrooms, thinly sliced

1 cloves garlic, finely chopped

1½ Tbsp nutritional yeast

Kosher salt and pepper

1 scallion, thinly sliced

Directions: Cook linguine per pkg. directions, reserving ½ cup pasta water. Drain and return to pot.

Meanwhile, heat oil in a large skillet on medium-high. Add mushrooms and cook, tossing often, until barely tender, about 5 minutes. Add garlic and cook, tossing, for 1 minute.

Toss hot pasta with nutritional yeast, ¼ cup reserved water, and ½ tsp salt to coat, adding additional pasta water as necessary. Toss with ¾ tsp coarsely cracked pepper, then mushrooms. Serve sprinkled with sliced scallion.

PER SERVING: 430 cal, 15 g pro, 62 g carb, 5 g fiber, 4 g sugars (0 g added sugars), 15 g fat (2 g sat fat), 0 mg chol, 175 mg sodium

Tofu Pad Thai

This lighter version of the takeout favorite gets its flavor from a mix of sweet chili sauce, garlic, brown sugar, and lime juice. Bonus: It takes just 35 minutes to make!

ACTIVE 25 MIN. | TOTAL 35 MIN. SERVES 2

- ½ 14-oz block extra-firm tofu
- 1 Tbsp cornstarch
- 4 oz rice noodles
- 2 Tbsp low-sodium soy sauce
- 1 Tbsp brown sugar
- 1 tsp sweet chili sauce
- Juice of ½ lime
- 1 small clove garlic, grated
- 1 Tbsp canola oil
- ½ red bell pepper, sliced
- 1 cup bean sprouts
- 1 scallion, thinly sliced, plus more for serving
- Chopped peanuts, for serving
- Lime wedges, for serving

Directions: Bring a medium pot of water to a boil. Slice the tofu ½ in. thick and place between paper towels on a rimmed baking sheet. Top with a second baking sheet and place a cast-iron skillet on top to weigh it down for 10 minutes. Cut into cubes and toss with the cornstarch.

Meanwhile, cook the noodles in the boiling water according to pkg. directions, then rinse. In a small bowl, combine the soy sauce, brown sugar, sweet chili sauce, lime juice, and garlic; set aside.

Heat the oil in a large nonstick skillet on medium. Add the pepper and cook until tender, 4 to 5 minutes. Remove from the skillet.

Add the tofu and cook, tossing, until golden brown, 4 to 5 minutes. Add noodles and sauce and toss to combine. Fold in the pepper, bean sprouts, and scallion; cook 2 minutes. Serve with the peanuts, lime wedges, and more scallions.

PER SERVING: 465 cal, 24 g pro, 52 g carb, 3 g fiber, 4 g sugars (2 g added sugars), 18 g fat (1.5 g sat fat), 43 mg chol, 624 mg sodium

Spiced Cod with Rice Noodle Salad

Cod is a rich source of omega-3 fats, a nutrient that supports the heart in a number of ways, including decreasing inflammation and triglycerides.

ACTIVE 25 MIN. | TOTAL 25 MIN.
SERVES 2

- 4 oz rice vermicelli noodles
- ½ cup snow peas, sliced lengthwise
- 1½ Tbsp fresh lime juice
- ½ Tbsp fish sauce
- 1 tsp sugar
- ½ red chile, seeded and thinly sliced
- 2 Tbsp oil
- ½ Tbsp grated fresh ginger
- ¼ tsp ground turmeric
- 8 oz skinless cod fillet (in large chunks)
- Kosher salt and pepper
- 2 Tbsp chopped dill
- 1 scallion, thinly sliced
- 1 Tbsp chopped peanuts, for serving

Directions: Cook noodles per pkg. directions, adding snow peas during last minute of cooking; drain and rinse in cold water.

In small bowl, mix lime juice, fish sauce, sugar, and ½ tsp water; stir in red chile. Toss half of sauce with noodles and snow peas.

In large bowl, mix oil, ginger, and turmeric. Toss with cod, then season with ¼ tsp each kosher salt and pepper.

Cook fish in nonstick skillet on medium, turning occasionally, until opaque throughout, 4 to 5 minutes. Sprinkle with dill and scallion. Serve over noodles with remaining dressing; top with chopped peanuts.

PER SERVING: 465 cal, 24 g pro, 52 g carb, 3 g fiber, 4 g sugars (2 g added sugars), 18 g fat (1.5 g sat fat), 43 mg chol, 624 mg sodium

Spicy Veggie Sauté

Your heart will thank you no matter what leafy green you choose for this dish. Spinach, kale, and Swiss chard are all rich in nitrates, a nutrient superstar that helps blood vessels expand and contract just the way healthy vessels should.

ACTIVE 10 MIN.
TOTAL 10 MIN.
SERVES 2

- ½ Tbsp olive oil
- ¼ tsp crushed red pepper flakes
- 4 cups spinach, kale, or Swiss chard
- 2 poached eggs
- 2 slices whole-wheat toast and 4 kiwis, for serving

Directions: Heat oil and crushed red pepper in a large skillet on medium for 1 minute. Add greens and cook, tossing until beginning to wilt, 1 to 3 minutes.

Transfer to plates and top with egg. Serve with toast and kiwis, if desired.

Tip: Transfer egg to an airtight container and cover with ice water. Refrigerate for several days. When ready to eat, transfer to a cup, cover with hot water and let sit until heated through, about 30 seconds.

PER SERVING: 345 cal, 17 g pro, 46 g carb, 10 g fiber, 0 g sugars (0 g added sugars), 13 g fat (3 g sat fat), 186 mg chol, 262 mg sodium

Lemon-Marinated Herb Pasta Salad

This zesty dish is the ideal make-ahead meal—it gets more flavorful as it sits!

**ACTIVE 20 MIN. | TOTAL 25 MIN.
SERVES 2**

4 oz short pasta, such as rotini
2 Tbsp olive oil
1 tsp lemon zest plus
½ Tbsp juice
Kosher salt and pepper
2 cups spinach
½ cup mixed fresh herbs
(basil, parsley, dill, chives)
¼ cup shaved Parmesan

Directions: Cook pasta per pkg. directions, rinse under cold water to cool, then drain well.

Meanwhile, in a large bowl, whisk together oil, lemon zest and juice, and ¼ tsp each salt and pepper. Toss with pasta and refrigerate until ready to serve (up to overnight).

When ready to serve, toss with spinach, herbs, and half of Parmesan. Serve with remaining Parmesan.

PER SERVING: 395 cal, 13 g pro, 45 g carb, 3 g fiber, 2 g sugars (0 g added sugars), 18.5 g fat (4.5 g sat fat), 13 mg chol, 475 mg sodium

WEEK 3 AT-A-GLANCE

DAY 15

Breakfast	🍴 Green Berry Smoothie Bowl
Snack	1 pear + 1 tsp cinnamon + ¼ cup low-fat ricotta
Lunch	♻ Spiced Cod with Rice Noodle Salad
Snack	Vegan Queso with 1 sliced red bell pepper
Dinner	Slow Cooker Butternut Squash Stew

DAY 16

Breakfast	♻ Spicy Veggie Sauté
Snack	2 pitted medjool dates with 1 Tbsp almond butter
Lunch	♻ Lemon-Marinated Herb Pasta Salad + ♻ Steamed Broccoli
Snack	Banana Bread Smoothie
Dinner	Smoky Vegan Black Bean Soup + 1 corn tortilla

DAY 17

Breakfast	2 egg whites, scrambled + Apple Chia Pudding
Snack	½ cup shelled edamame
Lunch	Tomato Bean Stuffed Potato
Snack	1 pear + 1 tsp cinnamon + ¼ cup low-fat ricotta
Dinner	♻ Slow Cooker Butternut Squash Stew

DAY 18

Breakfast	Chocolate Protein Smoothie
Snack	1 cup steamed or blanched broccoli with 2 Tbsp hummus + ½ cup shelled edamame
Lunch	♻ Smoky Vegan Black Bean Soup + 1 corn tortilla
Snack	2 pitted medjool dates + 1 Tbsp almond butter
Dinner	Roasted Cumin Shrimp and Asparagus

DAY 19

Breakfast	♻ 2 egg whites, scrambled + Apple Chia Pudding
Snack	1 cup steamed or blanched broccoli with 2 Tbsp hummus + ½ cup shelled edamame
Lunch	♻ Tomato Bean Stuffed Potato
Snack	🍴 Cherry Chocolate Nice Cream
Dinner	Pressure Cooker Winter Squash and Lentil Stew

DAY 20

Breakfast	♻ Chocolate Protein Smoothie
Snack	2 pitted medjool dates with 1 Tbsp almond butter
Lunch	♻ Roasted Cumin Shrimp and Asparagus
Snack	🍴 Cherry Chocolate Nice Cream
Dinner	Balsamic Chicken with Apple, Lentil, and Spinach Salad

DAY 21

Breakfast	♻ 2 egg whites, scrambled + Apple Chia Pudding
Snack	🍴 Cherry Chocolate Nice Cream
Lunch	♻ Pressure Cooker Winter Squash and Lentil Stew
Snack	1 cup steamed or blanched broccoli and 2 Tbsp hummus + ½ cup shelled edamame
Dinner	BBQ Chickpea and Grilled Nectarine Salad (p. 105) + Classic Quinoa

Key:

🍴 Meal Prep

♻ Leftover

WEEK 3
Shopping List

Buy Just What You Need

Below are exact amounts of every ingredient you will need for Week 3. Check for leftover ingredients from Week 2 before purchasing new ingredients from the list.

PRODUCE

- [ ] 3 apples
- [ ] 3 cups baby arugula
- [ ] 8 oz asparagus
- [ ] Avocado chunks, for serving
- [ ] 1 banana
- [ ] 1 sliced red bell pepper
- [ ] 3 cups broccoli
- [ ] ½ butternut squash
- [ ] 1 small carrot
- [ ] 1¼ stalks celery
- [ ] 2 Tbsp chopped cilantro, plus more for serving
- [ ] 6 cloves garlic
- [ ] ½ Tbsp grated fresh ginger
- [ ] ¼ green apple
- [ ] 1 stalk green onion
- [ ] ½ Tbsp lemon juice
- [ ] 1 lime
- [ ] ½ navel orange
- [ ] 2 nectarines
- [ ] 1 small onion
- [ ] 2 Tbsp flat-leaf parsley
- [ ] 2 pears
- [ ] ¾ red onion
- [ ] ½ scallion
- [ ] 1 shallot
- [ ] 12 cups baby spinach
- [ ] 2 sweet potatoes

- [ ] Assorted vegetables, such as carrot sticks and broccoli, for dipping

MEAT & SEAFOOD

- [ ] 1 6-oz boneless, skinless chicken breast
- [ ] 10 large peeled and deveined shrimp

REFRIGERATOR AND DAIRY

- [ ] 5½ cups unsweetened almond milk
- [ ] 6 eggs
- [ ] 6 Tbsp hummus
- [ ] ½ cup low-fat ricotta
- [ ] Shaved Parmesan, for serving

FROZEN

- [ ] 2 frozen bananas
- [ ] 2 cups frozen cauliflower
- [ ] 1½ cups frozen cherries
- [ ] ⅓ cup frozen corn
- [ ] 2 cups edamame

PANTRY

- [ ] 3 Tbsp almond butter
- [ ] 2½ Tbsp balsamic vinegar
- [ ] 2½ cups low-sodium canned black beans
- [ ] 1½ Tbsp light brown sugar
- [ ] ⅛ tsp ground cardamom
- [ ] 1 cup raw cashews

- [ ] ¼ tsp cayenne
- [ ] ½ cup chia seeds
- [ ] 2 cups low-sodium chicken or vegetable broth
- [ ] 3⅔ cups low-sodium canned chickpeas
- [ ] 2 tsp cider vinegar
- [ ] 5⅛ tsp cinnamon
- [ ] 1½ Tbsp chili powder
- [ ] 4½ Tbsp cocoa powder
- [ ] 1½ tsp ground coriander
- [ ] 1 cup couscous
- [ ] 3¾ tsp cumin
- [ ] 2 Tbsp ground flaxseed
- [ ] ½ cup canned lentils
- [ ] ⅓ lb green lentils
- [ ] 14 pitted medjool dates
- [ ] ¾ tsp ground ginger
- [ ] 2 Tbsp maple syrup
- [ ] ¼ cup rolled oats
- [ ] 6½ Tbsp olive oil
- [ ] ½ tsp smoked paprika
- [ ] ½ cup quinoa
- [ ] ¼ cup raisins
- [ ] 1 cup low-sodium crushed tomatoes
- [ ] 1 14.5-oz can whole tomatoes
- [ ] 1 Tbsp tomato paste
- [ ] 2 corn tortillas
- [ ] 1 tsp ground turmeric
- [ ] 1 Tbsp nutritional yeast

DAY 15: MEAL PLAN

Breakfast	Green Berry Smoothie Bowl Remove from freezer and set on counter first thing in the morning.
Snack	1 pear with 1 tsp cinnamon and ¼ cup low-fat ricotta
Lunch	Spiced Cod with Rice Noodle Salad
Snack	Vegan Queso (p. 99) with 1 sliced red bell pepper
Dinner	Slow Cooker Butternut Squash Stew (p. 99) Refrigerate remaining in airtight container for Day 17 dinner.

WATER INTAKE

MOVEMENT/WORKOUT

☐ Yes ☐ No

Activity: _____

_____

Duration: _____

Intensity: _____

SLEEP

Bedtime Last Night: _____

Wake Time This Morning: _____

Mood: 😒 😑 🥴 😐 😄

DAILY NUTRITION: 1,602 cal, 63 g pro, 271 g carb, 46 g fiber, 39 g fat (4 g sat fat), 58 mg chol, 1,724 mg sodium

DAY 16: MEAL PLAN

Breakfast	⟳ Spicy Veggie Sauté
Snack	2 pitted medjool dates + 1 Tbsp almond butter
Lunch	⟳ Lemon-Marinated Herb Pasta Salad + ⟳ Steamed Broccoli
Snack	Banana Bread Smoothie: Blend 1 frozen **banana**, ¾ cup **unsweetened almond milk**, ½ cup rinsed **low-sodium chickpeas**, ¼ cup **rolled oats**, 1 **pitted medjool date**, ½ tsp **vanilla extract**, and ¼ tsp **cinnamon** until smooth. Add more milk, if needed. Serves 1.
Dinner	Smoky Vegan Black Bean Soup (p. 100) + 1 corn tortilla. Refrigerate remaining in airtight container for Day 18 lunch.

WATER INTAKE

MOVEMENT/WORKOUT

☐ Yes ☐ No

Activity: _____

_____

Duration: _____

Intensity: _____

SLEEP

Bedtime Last Night: _____

Wake Time This Morning: _____

Mood: 😟 😣 🤪 😐 😄

DAILY NUTRITION: 1,739 cal, 66 g pro, 264 g carb, 53 g fiber, 55 g fat (10.5 g sat fat), 199 mg chol, 1,332 mg sodium

DAY 17: MEAL PLAN

Breakfast	2 egg whites, scrambled + Apple Chia Pudding
	In a pot over medium low heat, mix together ½ cup **chia seeds**, 2¼ cups **unsweetened almond milk**, ¾ tsp **cinnamon**, 3 **apples**, diced, and 2 Tbsp **maple syrup**. Stir until heated through and thickened, about 5 to 7 minutes. Serves 3.
	Refrigerate remaining pudding in airtight container for Day 19 and 21 breakfasts.
Snack	½ cup shelled edamame
Lunch	Tomato Bean Stuffed Potato: Cut 2 **sweet potatoes** in half and bake, flesh-side down, at 425°F for 20 to 30 minutes or until fork tender. Over medium-high heat, sauté 1 clove minced **garlic** and ⅔ **small onion**, chopped, in 2 Tbsp **balsamic vinegar** until soft. Add 1⅔ cups **low-sodium chickpeas** and 1 cup low-sodium **crushed tomatoes** for 5 minutes. Top each potato half with tomato bean mixture and garnish with 1 stalk sliced **green onion**. Serves 2.
	Refrigerate remaining in airtight container for Day 19 lunch.
Snack	1 pear + 1 tsp cinnamon + ¼ cup low-fat ricotta
Dinner	⟳ Slow Cooker Butternut Squash Stew

WATER INTAKE

MOVEMENT/WORKOUT

☐ Yes ☐ No

Activity: _____

Duration: _____

Intensity: _____

SLEEP

Bedtime Last Night: _____

Wake Time This Morning: _____

Mood: 😟 😕 😵 😐 😄

Meal Prep

MAKE

■ **Cherry Chocolate Nice Cream:** Blend 1½ cups **frozen cherries**, 3 **medjool dates**, 2¼ Tbsp **cocoa powder**, and ½ cup **unsweetened almond milk** until smooth. Add 1 splash of almond milk at a time if needed to achieve desired consistency. Serves 3.

STORE

Freeze 2 very ripe bananas for Chocolate Protein Smoothie.

DAILY NUTRITION: 1,486 cal, 62 g pro, 269 g carb, 57 g fiber, 26.5 g fat (1 g sat fat), 15 mg chol, 1,322 mg sodium

DAY 18: MEAL PLAN

Breakfast	Chocolate Protein Smoothie Blend 2 frozen **bananas**, 2 cups frozen **cauliflower**, 2 cups **unsweetened almond milk**, 1 cup **low-sodium black beans**, 2 Tbsp ground **flaxseed**, 2 Tbsp **cocoa powder**, 2 tsp **cinnamon**, and 4 pitted **dates** until smooth. Serves 2. Freeze remaining in an ice cube tray for Day 20 breakfast. Reblend when ready to eat.
Snack	1 cup steamed or blanched broccoli and 2 Tbsp hummus + ½ cup shelled edamame
Lunch	↻ Smoky Vegan Black Bean Soup + 1 corn tortilla
Snack	2 pitted medjool dates + 1 Tbsp almond butter
Dinner	Roasted Cumin Shrimp and Asparagus (p. 101) Refrigerate remaining in airtight container for Day 20 lunch.

WATER INTAKE

MOVEMENT/WORKOUT
☐ Yes ☐ No

Activity: _____

_____

Duration: _____

Intensity: _____

SLEEP
Bedtime Last Night: _____

Wake Time This Morning: _____

Mood: 😴 😒 🤢 😐 😄

DAILY NUTRITION: 1,420 cal, 60 g pro, 223 g carb, 58 g fiber, 42 g fat (5 g sat fat), 58 mg chol, 1,221 mg sodium

DAY 19: MEAL PLAN

Breakfast	2 egg whites, scrambled + 🔄 Apple Chia Pudding
Snack	1 cup steamed or blanched broccoli with 2 Tbsp hummus + ½ cup shelled edamame
Lunch	Tomato Bean Stuffed Potato: Cut 2 **sweet potatoes** in half and bake, flesh-side down, at 425°F for 20 to 30 minutes or until fork tender. Over medium-high heat, sauté 1 clove minced **garlic** and ⅔ **small onion**, chopped, in 2 Tbsp **balsamic vinegar** until soft. Add 1⅔ cups **low-sodium chickpeas** and 1 cup low-sodium **crushed tomatoes** and cook for 5 minutes. Top each potato half with tomato bean mixture and garnish with 1 stalk sliced **green onion**. Serves 2. Refrigerate remaining in airtight container for Day 19 lunch.
Snack	🍦 Cherry Chocolate Nice Cream
Dinner	Pressure Cooker Winter Squash and Lentil Stew (p. 103) Refrigerate remaining in airtight container for Day 21 lunch.

WATER INTAKE

MOVEMENT/WORKOUT

☐ Yes ☐ No

Activity: _____

_____

Duration: _____

Intensity: _____

SLEEP

Bedtime Last Night: _____

Wake Time This Morning: _____

Mood: 😔 😒 🤭 😐 😄

DAILY NUTRITION: 1,496 cal, 72 g pro, 239 g carb, 59 g fiber, 38 g fat (2.5 g sat fat), 0 mg chol, 1,334 mg sodium

DAY 20: MEAL PLAN

Breakfast	♻ Chocolate Protein Smoothie Remove from freezer first thing in the morning to thaw.
Snack	2 pitted medjool dates + 1 Tbsp almond butter
Lunch	♻ Roasted Cumin Shrimp and Asparagus
Snack	🍦 Cherry Chocolate Nice Cream
Dinner	Balsamic Chicken with Apple, Lentil, and Spinach Salad (p. 102)

WATER INTAKE

MOVEMENT/WORKOUT

☐ Yes ☐ No

Activity: _____

_____

Duration: _____

Intensity: _____

SLEEP

Bedtime Last Night: _____

Wake Time This Morning: _____

Mood: 😔 😣 🤧 😐 😄

DAILY NUTRITION: 1,425 cal, 78 g pro, 202 g carb, 48 g fiber, 42 g fat (6 g sat fat), 152 mg chol, 1,120 mg sodium

DAY 21: MEAL PLAN

Breakfast	2 egg whites, scrambled + ⟳ Apple Chia Pudding
Snack	ⓘ Cherry Chocolate Nice Cream
Lunch	⟳ Pressure Cooker Winter Squash and Lentil Stew
Snack	1 cup steamed or blanched broccoli and 2 Tbsp hummus + ½ cup shelled edamame
Dinner	BBQ Chickpea and Grilled Nectarine Salad (p. 105) + Classic Quinoa Cook ½ cup **quinoa** in ¾ cup **low-sodium vegetable broth** according to pkg. directions. Serves 2. Refrigerate remaining in airtight container for Day 23 lunch.

WATER INTAKE

MOVEMENT/WORKOUT

☐ Yes ☐ No

Activity: _____

_____

Duration: _____

Intensity: _____

SLEEP

Bedtime Last Night:

_____

Wake Time This Morning:

_____

Mood: 🙂

Meal Prep

MAKE

■ **Chili Lime Roasted Chickpeas:** Drain and rinse 3 cups low-sodium **chickpeas**. Spread out on absorbent towel, cover with second towel, and roll around until very dry. Transfer to bowl and mix well with the juice and zest of 1 **lime**, 2 tsp **chili powder**, ⅔ tsp **salt**, and ⅓ tsp **black pepper**. Roast at 350°F for 35 to 40 minutes, shaking baking sheet every 10 minutes or so. Serves 4.

■ **Dairy-Free Tzatziki with Broccoli:** In a bowl, combine 1 cup **unsweetened coconut yogurt**, ⅓ grated **cucumber**, and 1 Tbsp **lemon juice**. Blanch 4 cups **broccoli** by boiling a pot of water and boiling broccoli for 1 to 2 minutes. Remove broccoli with slotted spoon and quickly place in a bowl of water and ice. Serves 4.

Refrigerate in airtight container for Day 22, 23, 24, and 25 snacks.

■ **1 hard-boiled egg**

DAILY NUTRITION: 1,563 cal, 69 g pro, 227 g carb, 52 g fiber, 53 g fat (4.5 g sat fat), 0 mg chol, 1,356 mg sodium

Citrus-Pineapple Bowl

Smoothie bowls are a quick way to get a jump-start on your fruit intake for the day. This one is packed with pineapple, oranges, and grapefruit.

ACTIVE 5 MIN. | TOTAL 10 MIN.
SERVES 2

FOR SMOOTHIE
½ cup fat-free Greek yogurt
½ cup frozen pineapple
1 tsp vanilla extract
½ navel orange, segmented
¼ Ruby Red grapefruit, segmented

FOR TOPPING
¼ cup fat-free Greek yogurt
2 Tbsp raw cashews, coarsely chopped
2 Tbsp unsweetened coconut
2 tsp chia seeds
½ navel orange, segmented
¼ Ruby Red grapefruit, segmented

Directions: Puree all smoothie ingredients in blender until creamy.

Divide between 2 bowls then top with remaining ingredients.

PER SERVING: 240 cal, 12 g pro, 31 g carb, 5 g fiber, 19 g sugars (0 added sugars), 8 g fat (4 g sat fat), 4 mg chol, 34 mg sodium

Vegan Queso

Nutritional yeast is the perfect heart-healthy swap when you have a craving for something cheesy. It's a wonderful source of beta-glucan, a type of fiber known for its cholesterol-lowering powers.

ACTIVE 15 MIN. | TOTAL 30 MIN.
SERVES 2

1 Tbsp olive oil
4 cloves garlic, pressed
1 cup raw cashews
1½ Tbsp chili powder
2 tsp ground cumin
1 tsp ground coriander
1 tsp ground turmeric
⅛ to ¼ tsp cayenne
Kosher salt and pepper
¼ cup nutritional yeast
Chopped cilantro and vegetables, for serving

Directions: Heat oil and garlic in small saucepan on medium until sizzling, about 1 minute. Stir in cashews, then spices and ½ tsp each salt and pepper. Add 1½ cups water and bring mixture to a boil. Reduce heat and simmer until cashews are softened, 12 to 14 minutes.

Transfer mixture to blender, add nutritional yeast and ½ cup water, and puree until smooth.

Return mixture to saucepan on medium-low and cook, stirring occasionally, until thickened, 6 to 8 minutes. Transfer to bowl. Top with cilantro and serve with vegetables, if desired.

PER SERVING: Per serving: 120 cal, 5 g pro, 8 g carb, 2 g fiber, 1 g sugars (0 g added sugars), 8.5 g fat (1.5 g sat fat), 0 mg chol, 175 mg sodium

Slow Cooker Butternut Squash Stew

Butternut squash is a delicious low-glycemic veggie—that means it gets digested slowly and helps keep blood sugar levels under control.

ACTIVE 20 MIN.
TOTAL 7 HR. 0 MIN.
SERVES 2

1 14.5-oz can whole tomatoes
¼ cup raisins
1 tsp ground cumin
¾ tsp ground ginger
⅛ tsp ground cinnamon
Kosher salt and pepper
½ red onion
¼ medium butternut squash
½ cup couscous
2 Tbsp chopped cilantro
½ 15-oz can chickpeas, rinsed

Directions: In a 5- to 6-qt slow cooker, add tomatoes (and their juices), breaking them with your hands as you add them. Stir in raisins, cumin, ginger, cinnamon, and ¼ tsp each salt and pepper.

Add onion and squash and cook, covered, until squash is tender, 5 to 7 hr. on Low or 3 to 5 hr. on High.

Ten minutes before serving, cook couscous per pkg. directions; fold in cilantro.

Gently fold the chickpeas into the stew and cook, covered, until heated through, about 3 minutes. Serve stew over couscous.

PER SERVING: 440 cal, 15 g pro, 94 g carb, 13 g fiber, 24 g sugars (0 g added sugars), 2.5 g fat (0 g sat fat), 0 mg chol, 700 mg sodium

Smoky Vegan Black Bean Soup

This wholesome, cholesterol-free soup is hearty enough to enjoy for dinner—it serves up 14 g of filling protein and 19 g of fiber per serving!

ACTIVE 20 MIN. | TOTAL 4 HR. 50 MIN. | SERVES 2

- **1 Tbsp olive oil**
- **1 small onion, finely chopped**
- **1 small carrot, cut into ¼-in. pieces**
- **1 small stalk celery, sliced**
- **1 Tbsp tomato paste**
- **1 clove garlic, finely chopped**
- **½ tsp ground cumin**
- **¼ tsp smoked paprika**
- **3 cups low-sodium vegetable broth**
- **1 15-oz can low-sodium black beans, rinsed**
- **⅓ cup frozen corn**
- **Avocado chunks and cilantro, for serving**

Directions: Heat oil in a Dutch oven on medium. Add onion, carrot, and celery and cook, covered, stirring occasionally, until just tender, 8 to 10 minutes. Stir in tomato paste, garlic, cumin and paprika and cook, stirring until tomato paste darkens, 1 to 2 minutes.

Stir in broth and cook, scraping up any brown bits. Add beans and corn and simmer for 15 minutes. Serve topped with avocado and cilantro.

PER SERVING: 305 cal, 13 g pro, 47 g carb, 16 g fiber, 7 g sugars (0 g added sugars), 8 g fat (1 g sat fat), 0 mg chol, 400 mg sodium

Roasted Cumin
Shrimp and Asparagus

Oranges aren't the only way to get your vitamin C. Asparagus is also an excellent source of this mighty micronutrient, which has been linked to lower blood pressure levels.

ACTIVE 15 MIN.
TOTAL 30 MIN.
SERVES 2

½ cup couscous
½ orange, divided
Kosher salt and pepper
8 oz asparagus
½ Tbsp olive oil
10 large peeled and deveined shrimp
¼ tsp ground cumin
⅛ tsp cayenne

Directions: Bring ¾ cup water to a boil. Place the couscous in bowl. Top with juice of ¼ orange, then add ½ cup hot water. Cover and let sit 10 minutes, then fluff and season with salt and pepper.

Meanwhile, heat the broiler. On a rimmed baking sheet, toss asparagus with oil, then season with salt and pepper to taste. Broil 3 minutes.

Season shrimp with cumin, cayenne, and ⅛ tsp salt and arrange on sheet with asparagus. Broil until shrimp are just opaque throughout and the asparagus is just tender, 3 to 4 minutes more.

Squeeze remaining ¼ orange over the shrimp and asparagus and serve with couscous.

PER SERVING: 270 cal, 12 g pro, 39 g carb, 4 g fiber, 3 g sugars (0 g added sugars), 7.5 g fat (1 g sat fat), 58 mg chol, 445 mg sodium

Balsamic Chicken with Apple, Lentil, and Spinach Salad

This dish is full of flavor (and heart-healthy fiber) thanks to the balanced combination of tart balsamic chicken and a lightly sweet and crunchy salad made with celery, green apple, and lemon juice.

ACTIVE 15 MIN. | TOTAL 25 MIN. | SERVES 1

1 Tbsp olive oil
1 6-oz boneless, skinless chicken breast
Kosher salt and pepper
½ Tbsp balsamic vinegar
½ scallion, thinly sliced
¼ green apple, cut into small pieces
¼ stalk celery, thinly sliced
½ Tbsp fresh lemon juice
½ cup canned lentils, rinsed
½ cup baby spinach, roughly chopped
2 Tbsp fresh flat-leaf parsley, roughly chopped

Directions: Heat ½ Tbsp oil in a small skillet over medium heat. Season the chicken with pinch each salt and pepper and cook until golden brown and cooked through, 8 to 10 minutes per side. Remove from heat and add the vinegar. Turn the chicken to coat.

Meanwhile, in a large bowl, toss the scallion, apple, celery, lemon juice, remaining ½ Tbsp oil, and a pinch each salt and pepper. Fold in lentils, spinach, and parsley. Serve with chicken.

PER SERVING: 450 cal, 44 g pro, 27 g carb, 11 g fiber, 8 g sugars (0 g added sugars), 17.5 g fat (3 g sat fat), 94 mg chol, 444 mg sodium

Prefer stovetop?
You can make this dish in a saucepan or Dutch oven instead. Stir in lentils and broth and simmer, partially covered, stirring occasionally, until tender, 15 to 20 minutes.

Pressure Cooker Winter Squash and Lentil Stew

Lentils are like mini nutrient machines, packed with iron, protein, and cholesterol-lowering fiber. They add earthy flavor to this cold-weather stew.

ACTIVE 20 MIN. | TOTAL 35 MIN. SERVES 2

- **1 Tbsp olive oil**
- **1 shallot, thinly sliced**
- **½ Tbsp grated fresh ginger**
- **½ tsp ground coriander**
- **⅛ tsp ground cardamom**
- **½ small butternut squash (neck only) peeled and cut into 1½-in. pieces**
- **⅓ lb green lentils, picked over**
- **2 cups low-sodium chicken or vegetable broth**
- **2 tsp cider vinegar**
- **2 cups packed baby spinach**

Directions: Set an electric pressure cooker to Sauté and adjust to medium. Add oil, shallots, and ginger and cook, stirring occasionally until shallots are golden brown, 3 to 5 minutes. Stir in coriander and cardamom and cook, stirring, for 1 minute.

Add squash, lentils, broth, and ¼ tsp salt. Cover and lock lid. Cook on high pressure for 12 minutes.

Use quick-release method to release pressure. Uncover and stir in vinegar and ¼ tsp each salt and pepper, then stir in spinach to wilt.

PER SERVING: 390 cal, 25 g pro, 58 g carb, 14 g fiber, 6 g sugars (0 g added sugars), 9 g fat (1.5 g sat fat), 0 mg chol, 595 mg sodium

BBQ Chickpea and Grilled Nectarine Salad

This easy salad's got it all: smoky chickpeas, sweet charred nectarines, and fresh peppery arugula. A healthy serving of Parmesan cheese on top brings it all together.

**ACTIVE 25 MIN. | TOTAL 25 MIN.
SERVES 2**

¼ **small red onion, thinly sliced**
2 **Tbsp fresh lime juice**
½ **15.5-oz can chickpeas,
rinsed**
2 **Tbsp olive oil, divided**
¼ **tsp smoked paprika**
1½ **Tbsp light brown sugar,
divided**
¼ **tsp chili powder, divided**
2 **nectarines, pitted,
each cut into 6 wedges**
Kosher salt and pepper
3 **cups baby arugula**
Shaved Parmesan, for serving

Directions: Heat grill on medium. In large bowl, toss onion with lime juice; let sit, tossing occasionally.

In second bowl, toss chickpeas with ½ Tbsp oil, then smoked paprika, 1 Tbsp brown sugar, and ⅛ tsp chili powder. Transfer to medium cast-iron skillet and cook on grill, stirring occasionally, until crisp, 12 to 14 minutes.

Toss nectarines with ½ Tbsp oil and grill until lightly charred, about 3 minutes per side.

To bowl with onions, whisk in remaining Tbsp oil, ½ Tbsp brown sugar, ⅛ tsp chili powder, and ⅛ tsp each salt and pepper. Gently toss with arugula and fold in apricots and chickpeas. Serve topped with shaved Parmesan if desired.

*PER SERVING: 335 cal, 8 g pro, 45 g carb, 8 g fiber,
26 g sugars (10 g added sugars), 16 g fat (2 g sat fat),
0 mg chol, 295 mg sodium*

WEEK 4 AT-A-GLANCE

DAY 22

Breakfast	Citrus-Pineapple Bowl
Snack	🍴 1 hard-boiled egg + 🍴 Dairy-Free Tzatziki with Blanched Broccoli
Lunch	Smashed Chickpea Salad Sandwich + 1 orange
Snack	🍴 Chili Lime Roasted Chickpeas
Dinner	Supergreen Mushroom and Orzo Soup + Three-Bean Salad

DAY 23

Breakfast	Open-Faced Avocado Sandwich + 1 orange
Snack	🍴 Dairy-Free Tzatziki with Broccoli
Lunch	🔁 BBQ Chickpea and Grilled Nectarine Salad + Classic Quinoa
Snack	🍴 Chili Lime Roasted Chickpeas
Dinner	Sheet Pan Chicken Fajitas + Spicy Rice

DAY 24

Breakfast	🍴 Zucchini Bread Overnight Oats
Snack	🍴 Dairy-Free Tzatziki with Broccoli
Lunch	🔁 Smashed Chickpea Salad Sandwich + 1 orange
Snack	🍴 Chili Lime Roasted Chickpeas
Dinner	Pesto Pasta + Lemon Garlic Spinach

DAY 25

Breakfast	🔁 Citrus-Pineapple Bowl
Snack	🍴 Dairy-Free Tzatziki with Broccoli
Lunch	🔁 Sheet Pan Chicken Fajitas + 🔁 Spicy Rice
Snack	🍴 Garlic White Bean Dip with Sliced Cucumber
Dinner	Halibut with Potatoes and Brussels Sprouts

DAY 26

Breakfast	🍴 Zucchini Bread Overnight Oats
Snack	½ cup blueberries + 1 oz low-fat cheese
Lunch	🔁 Pesto Pasta + 🔁 Lemon Garlic Spinach
Snack	🍴 Garlic White Bean Dip with Sliced Cucumber
Dinner	Spicy Tofu Tacos + Rice and Pinto Beans

DAY 27

Breakfast	Open-Faced Avocado Sandwich + 1 orange
Snack	½ cup blueberries + 1 oz low-fat cheese
Lunch	Smashed Chickpea Salad Sandwich 🔁 + 1 orange
Snack	🍴 Garlic White Bean Dip with Sliced Cucumber
Dinner	🔁 Halibut with Potatoes and Brussels Sprouts

DAY 28

Breakfast	🍴 Zucchini Bread Overnight Oats
Snack	½ cup blueberries + 1 oz low-fat cheese
Lunch	🔁 Spicy Tofu Tacos + 🔁 Rice and Pinto Beans
Snack	🍴 Chili Lime Roasted Chickpeas
Dinner	Fiery Black Bean Soup + Savory Sautéed Kale

Key:

🍴 Meal Prep

🔁 Leftover

WEEK 4
Shopping List

Buy Just What You Need
Below are exact amounts of every ingredient you will need for Week 4. Check for leftover ingredients from Week 3 before purchasing new ingredients from the list.

PRODUCE

- ½ avocado
- 1 red bell pepper
- ½ yellow bell pepper
- 1½ cups blueberries
- 4½ cups broccoli
- ½ lb Brussels sprouts
- 1 carrot
- 2 stalks celery
- ⅓ cup cherry tomatoes
- Cilantro, for serving
- 1⅓ cucumbers
- 11½ cloves garlic
- ½ Ruby Red grapefruit
- 2 oz green/string beans
- 1 jalapeño plus more for slicing/serving
- 1 cup kale
- 1¾ lemons
- 2½ limes
- 3 mushrooms
- 2 onions
- 1 green onion
- 1 red onion
- 5 oranges
- 1 navel orange
- ¼ small pineapple
- 1½ poblano peppers
- ½ lb fingerling potatoes
- 2 radishes
- Shredded romaine lettuce, for serving
- ½ scallion
- 1 shallot
- 12 cups spinach
- 1 Tbsp thyme and rosemary (mixed)
- 2 cups grape tomatoes
- ½ lb tomatillos
- 1 medium zucchini

MEAT & SEAFOOD

- 2 6-oz boneless, skinless chicken breasts
- 2 6-oz pieces halibut fillet

REFRIGERATOR & DAIRY

- 1½ cups unsweetened almond milk
- 3 oz low-fat cheese
- 1 egg
- 7 oz extra-firm tofu
- ¾ cups fat-free Greek yogurt

FROZEN

- ½ cup frozen pineapple

BREAD AND BAKERY

- 6 slices whole-wheat bread
- 2 whole-grain English muffins

PANTRY

- 1 Tbsp adobo sauce
- 1⅔ cups 10-minute brown rice
- 2 15-oz cans low-sodium black beans
- 2 Tbsp raw cashews
- 2 tsp chia seeds
- 4¼ cups low-sodium chicken broth
- 4½ cups low-sodium canned chickpeas
- 3¾ tsp chili powder
- 1 tsp cinnamon
- 2 Tbsp unsweetened coconut
- 1½ tsp cumin
- ¾ tsp ground coriander
- 6 Tbsp ground flaxseed
- 1½ tsp garlic powder
- 2 Tbsp maple syrup
- 1½ Tbsp Dijon mustard
- ½ Tbsp nutritional yeast
- 1½ cups rolled oats
- 6½ Tbsp olive oil
- 1 Tbsp oil
- 1 tsp onion powder

DAY 22: MEAL PLAN

Breakfast	Citrus-Pineapple Bowl (p. 98) Freeze remaining in airtight container for Day 25 breakfast.
Snack	🍽 1 hard-boiled egg + 🍽 Dairy-Free Tzatziki with Broccoli
Lunch	Smashed Chickpea Salad Sandwich + 1 orange In a large bowl, roughly mash 1 cup **low-sodium canned chickpeas**, drained and rinsed, with a fork or potato masher. Mix in 1 stalk **celery**, 1 stalk **green onion**, diced, ⅓ cup grated **carrot**, ¼ cup **hummus**, 1½ Tbsp **Dijon mustard**, 1½ Tbsp **lemon juice**, ⅛ tsp **garlic powder**, and **salt** and **pepper** to taste. Spoon a third of the mixture between 2 slices of whole-wheat bread along with ½ cup **baby spinach**. Mixture serves 3. Refrigerate remaining and additional 1 cup spinach in airtight container for Day 24 and 27 lunches.
Snack	Chili Lime Roasted Chickpeas
Dinner	Supergreen Mushroom and Orzo Soup (p. 115) + Three-Bean Salad (p. 116)

WATER INTAKE

MOVEMENT/WORKOUT

☐ Yes ☐ No

Activity: _____

_____

Duration: _____

Intensity: _____

SLEEP

Bedtime Last Night: _____

Wake Time This Morning: _____

Mood: 😟 😣 🤧 😐 😄

DAILY NUTRITION: 1,527 cal, 66 g pro, 200 g carb, 49 g fiber, 56 g fat (12 g sat fat), 186 mg chol, 2,098 mg sodium

DAY 23: MEAL PLAN

Breakfast	Open-Faced Avocado Sandwich (p. 118) + 1 orange
Snack	Dairy-Free Tzatziki with Broccoli
Lunch	BBQ Chickpea and Grilled Nectarine Salad + Classic Quinoa
Snack	Chili Lime Roasted Chickpeas
Dinner	Sheet Pan Chicken Fajitas (p. 117) + Spicy Rice Cook 1 cup **brown rice** in ¾ cup **water** and ½ cup **low-sodium salsa**. Serves 2. Refrigerate remaining in airtight container for Day 25 lunch.

WATER INTAKE

MOVEMENT/WORKOUT

☐ Yes ☐ No

Activity: _____

_____

Duration: _____

Intensity: _____

Meal Prep

MAKE

■ **Zucchini Bread Overnight Oats:**
Combine in a large container:
1½ cups each **rolled oats** and
unsweetened almond milk, 6
Tbsp **ground flaxseed**, 2 Tbsp
maple syrup, 1 tsp **cinnamon**,
and 1 **medium zucchini**, grated.
Serves 3.

Refrigerate in 3 airtight
containers overnight for Day 24,
26, and 28 breakfasts.

SLEEP

Bedtime Last Night: _____

Wake Time This Morning: _____

Mood:

DAILY NUTRITION: 1,558 cal, 77 g pro, 228 g carb, 41 g fiber, 45 g fat (7.5 g sat fat), 94 mg chol, 1,587 mg sodium

DAY 24: MEAL PLAN

Breakfast	🍽 Zucchini Bread Overnight Oats
Snack	🍽 Dairy-Free Tzatziki with Broccoli
Lunch	🔁 Smashed Chickpea Salad Sandwich + 1 orange
Snack	🍽 Chili Lime Roasted Chickpeas
Dinner	Pesto Pasta (p. 118) + Lemon Garlic Spinach In 1 to 2 Tbsp **water** over medium-high heat, in batches, sauté 10 cups **baby spinach**, 3 cloves minced **garlic**, 1 Tbsp **lemon juice**, and ⅛ tsp **salt** (optional) until wilted. Serves 2. Refrigerate remaining in airtight container for Day 26 lunch.

WATER INTAKE

MOVEMENT/WORKOUT

☐ Yes ☐ No

Activity: _____

_____

Duration: _____

Intensity: _____

Meal Prep

MAKE

■ **Garlic White Bean Dip with Sliced Cucumber:** Blend 1½ cups **low-sodium white beans**, drained and rinsed, 1½ Tbsp **tahini**, 1½ Tbsp **lemon juice** + ¾ tsp **thyme**, ¼ tsp **garlic powder**, and 1 Tbsp **water** (or more if needed). Cut 1 **cucumber** into thin slices.
Serves 3.

Refrigerate in airtight container for Day 25, 26, and 27 snacks.

SLEEP

Bedtime Last Night: _____

Wake Time This Morning: _____

Mood: 😓 😒 🤢 😐 😄

DAILY NUTRITION: 1,386 cal, 58 g pro, 236 g carb, 46.5 g fiber, 31.5 g fat (5.5 g sat fat), 0 mg chol, 1,606 mg sodium

DAY 25: MEAL PLAN

Breakfast	⟳ Citrus-Pineapple Bowl Remove from freezer first thing in the morning to thaw.
Snack	🍴 Dairy-Free Tzatziki with Broccoli
Lunch	⟳ Sheet Pan Chicken Fajitas + ⟳ Spicy Rice
Snack	🍴 Garlic White Bean Dip with Sliced Cucumber
Dinner	Halibut with Potatoes and Brussels Sprouts (p. 120) Refrigerate remaining in airtight container for Day 27 dinner.

WATER INTAKE

MOVEMENT/WORKOUT

☐ Yes ☐ No

Activity: _____

_____

Duration: _____

Intensity: _____

SLEEP

Bedtime Last Night: _____

Wake Time This Morning: _____

Mood: 😣 😠 🤧 😐 😄

DAILY NUTRITION: 1,383 cal, 102 g pro, 163 g carb, 32 g fiber, 40 g fat (11 g sat fat), 177 mg chol, 1,054 mg sodium

DAY 26: MEAL PLAN

Breakfast	🍽 Zucchini Bread Overnight Oats
Snack	½ cup blueberries + 1 oz low-fat cheese
Lunch	🔄 Pesto Pasta + 🔄 Lemon Garlic Spinach
Snack	🍽 Garlic White Bean Dip with Sliced Cucumber
Dinner	Spicy Tofu Tacos (p. 119) + Rice and Pinto Beans Cook ⅔ cups each **10-minute brown rice** and **water** according to pkg. directions. In bowl, combine ⅔ cup **low-sodium pinto beans**, drained and rinsed, with 1 tsp each **chili powder**, **cumin**, **garlic powder**, **onion powder**, and **oregano**. Fold beans into rice. Serves 2. Refrigerate remaining in airtight container for Day 28 lunch.

WATER INTAKE

MOVEMENT/WORKOUT

☐ Yes ☐ No

Activity: _____

_____

Duration: _____

Intensity: _____

SLEEP

Bedtime Last Night: _____

Wake Time This Morning: _____

Mood: 😟 😕 🤪 😐 😄

DAILY NUTRITION: 1,449 cal, 66 g pro, 228 g carb, 43.5 g fiber, 41 g fat (7.5 g sat fat), 10 mg chol, 1,112 mg sodium

DAY 27: MEAL PLAN

Breakfast	Open-Faced Avocado Sandwich (p. 118) + 1 orange
Snack	½ cup blueberries + 1 oz low-fat cheese
Lunch	⟳ Smashed Chickpea Salad Sandwich + 1 orange
Snack	🍴 Garlic White Bean Dip with Sliced Cucumber
Dinner	⟳ Halibut with Potatoes and Brussels Sprouts

WATER INTAKE

MOVEMENT/WORKOUT

☐ Yes ☐ No

Activity: _____

_____

Duration: _____

Intensity: _____

SLEEP

Bedtime Last Night: _____

Wake Time This Morning: _____

Mood: 😔 😣 🤧 😐 😁

DAILY NUTRITION: 1,401 cal, 81 g pro, 194 g carb, 45 g fiber, 39 g fat (7 g sat fat), 93 mg chol, 1,434 mg sodium

DAY 28: MEAL PLAN

Breakfast	🍽 Zucchini Bread Overnight Oats
Snack	½ cup blueberries + 1 oz low-fat cheese
Lunch	🔁 Spicy Tofu Tacos + 🔁 Rice and Pinto Beans
Snack	🍽 Chili Lime Roasted Chickpeas
Dinner	Fiery Black Bean Soup (p. 123) + Savory Sautéed Kale In 1 to 2 Tbsp **water** over medium-low heat, sauté 2 cups chopped **kale** (tough stems removed), 1 Tbsp **nutritional yeast**, and 1 clove minced **garlic**. Season with **salt** (optional). Cover and simmer for 3 to 5 minutes or until desired doneness. Serves 2.

WATER INTAKE

MOVEMENT/WORKOUT

☐ Yes ☐ No

Activity: _____

_____

Duration: _____

Intensity: _____

SLEEP

Bedtime Last Night: _____

Wake Time This Morning: _____

Mood: 😔 😕 🥴 😐 😁

DAILY NUTRITION: 1,523 cal, 79 g pro, 235 g carb, 57 g fiber, 37.5 g fat (6 g sat fat), 10 mg chol, 1,833 mg sodium

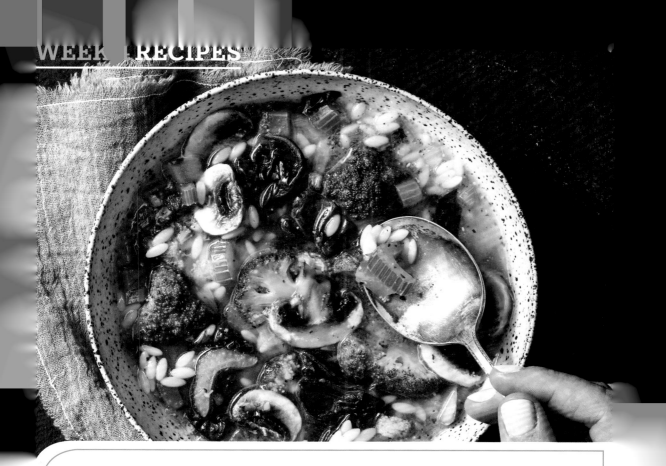

Supergreen Mushroom & Orzo Soup

Get a serious dose of green from this comforting one-pot soup.

**ACTIVE 25 MIN. | TOTAL 25 MIN.
SERVES 1**

- **1 Tbsp olive oil**
- **1 shallot, chopped**
- **½ small stalk celery, sliced**
- **Kosher salt and pepper**
- **1 small clove garlic, finely chopped**
- **1½ cups low-sodium vegetable or chicken broth**
- **3 Tbsp orzo**
- **½ cup broccoli florets**
- **3 mushrooms, sliced**
- **½ cup spinach, sliced**
- **½ to 1 Tbsp pesto**

Directions: Heat oil in a small saucepan on medium. Add shallot and celery, season with pinch each salt and pepper and sauté until beginning to turn golden brown, 6 to 8 minutes. Stir in garlic and cook 1 minute.

Add broth and orzo and bring to a simmer. Simmer for 6 minutes. Add broccoli and simmer 3 minutes. Stir in mushrooms and simmer until orzo and vegetables are just tender. Remove from heat and stir in spinach to wilt. Serve with a drizzle of pesto.

PER SERVING: 275 cal, 6 g pro, 22 g carb, 5 g fiber, 5 g sugars (0 g added sugars), 19 g fat (3 g sat fat), 0 mg chol, 535 mg sodium

Three-Bean Salad

A classic picnic dish gets an update with fresh flavors and a bright vinaigrette. One serving provides a whopping 8 grams of fiber, making it a heart-healthy staple.

ACTIVE 20 MIN. | TOTAL 20 MIN. SERVES 1

Kosher salt and pepper
2 oz green beans, trimmed
½ Tbsp olive oil
½ small clove garlic, finely grated
¼ cup cherry tomatoes
¼ tsp orange zest
¾ tsp orange juice
½ tsp white wine vinegar
¼ tsp toasted sesame oil
½ tsp toasted sesame seeds
Scant ¼ cup canned chickpeas, rinsed
Scant ¼ cup canned cannellini beans, rinsed
½ scallion, thinly sliced

Directions: Bring a large pot of water to boil. Add 1 tsp salt, then green beans, and simmer until crisp-tender, 3 minutes. Immediately transfer to a bowl of ice water to cool, about 5 minutes. Drain and pat dry.

Meanwhile, heat oil and garlic in a small skillet on medium for 1 minute. Stir in tomatoes and cook, tossing occasionally, until just beginning to split, 3 to 4 minutes.

Remove skillet from heat and toss with orange juice, vinegar, and sesame oil, then sesame seeds and orange zest.

In a large bowl, toss green beans with chickpeas, cannellini beans, and scallions, then toss with tomato mixture and pinch each salt and pepper.

PER SERVING: 220 cal, 9 g pro, 26 g carb, 10 g fiber, 5 g sugars (0 g added sugars), 10 g fat (1 g sat fat), 0 mg chol, 404 mg sodium

Sheet Pan Chicken Fajitas

Pineapple brightens this Mexican-style favorite, and adds loads of fiber, vitamin C, and potassium to boot.

ACTIVE 20 MIN. | TOTAL 40 MIN. SERVES 2

2 6-oz boneless, skinless chicken breasts
1 Tbsp adobo sauce
Kosher salt
½ red pepper, sliced
½ yellow pepper, sliced
½ onion, sliced
¼ small pineapple, cut into matchsticks
1 Tbsp olive oil
Lime wedges, for serving

Directions: Heat broiler. Toss chicken with adobo sauce and ¼ tsp kosher salt. Place on rimmed baking sheet and broil 6 minutes; transfer to plate. Lower oven temp to 425°F.

On same baking sheet, toss peppers, onion, and pineapple with olive oil and ¼ tsp salt. Roast 15 minutes.

Nestle chicken amid vegetables and roast until chicken is cooked through and vegetables are tender, 5 minutes more. Slice chicken and serve with vegetables and lime wedges.

PER SERVING: 310 cal, 36 g pro, 19 g carb, 3 g fiber, 11 g sugars (0.5 g added sugars), 10 g fat (2 g sat fat), 94 g chol, 355 mg sodium

Open-Faced Avocado Sandwich

Creamy avocado tastes decadent but is full of good-for-you monoun-saturated fats, the heart-healthy kind that can help lower cholesterol.

ACTIVE 5 MIN. | TOTAL 5 MIN.
SERVES 1

¼ sliced avocado
1 whole-grain English muffin
1 radish, sliced

Directions: Arrange avocado on English muffin halves. Top each half with radish.

PER SERVING: 215 cal, 7 g pro, 31 g carb, 8 g fiber, 6 g sugars (0 g added sugars), 9 g fat (1.5 g sat fat), 0 mg chol, 245 mg sodium

Pesto Pasta

Basil, one of the main ingredients in this dish's herby sauce, is packed with nitrates, an important nutrient that protects against heart disease.

ACTIVE 20 MIN. | TOTAL 20 MIN. | SERVES 2

1 cup penne
2 oz green beans, trimmed and cut in 1-in. pieces
¼ cup low-sodium chicken broth
2 Tbsp prepared pesto
2 cups grape tomatoes, halved

Directions: Cook penne per pkg. directions, adding green beans during last 3 minutes of cooking.

In a bowl, whisk together broth and pesto. Add pasta and beans and toss to combine. Fold in tomatoes.

PER SERVING: 285 cal, 10 g pro, 52 g carb, 4.5 g fiber, 4 g sugars (0 g added sugars), 7.5 g fat (1.5 g sat fat), 0 mg chol, 195 mg sodium

Spicy Tofu Tacos

Crumbling the tofu helps give these hearty tacos the texture of the classic ground beef version, while the seasoning mix packs all the flavor.

ACTIVE 20 MIN. | TOTAL 20 MIN.
SERVES 2

1 Tbsp oil
½ small poblano pepper, cut into ¼-in. pieces
½ red pepper, cut into ¼-in. pieces
½ small onion, chopped
1 clove garlic, finely chopped
½ 14-oz pkg. extra-firm tofu (squeeze out excess moisture)
¾ tsp chili powder
¼ tsp ground coriander
Kosher salt and pepper
4 corn tortillas
Shredded romaine lettuce and sliced jalapeno, for serving

Directions: Heat oil in a large skillet on medium. Add peppers and onion and sauté for 5 minutes. Stir in garlic and cook 1 minute.

Crumble tofu into skillet, season with chili powder, ground coriander, and ¼ tsp each salt and pepper, and cook, stirring occasionally, until golden brown.

Serve in tortillas topped with lettuce and jalapeno.

PER SERVING: 290 cal, 14 g pro, 30 g carb, 6 g fiber, 4 g sugars (0 g added sugars), 13.5 g fat (2 g sat fat), 0 mg chol, 300 mg sodium

Halibut with Potatoes and Brussels Sprouts

Load up on protein and veggies with this simple 35-minute meal.

ACTIVE 15 MIN. | TOTAL 35 MIN. | SERVES 2

½ lb fingerling potatoes (about 20), halved
½ lb Brussels sprouts (about 10), trimmed and quartered
1 shallot, cut into wedges
1½ Tbsp olive oil, divided
Kosher salt and pepper
2 6-oz pieces halibut fillet

Directions: Heat oven to 425°F. On a rimmed baking sheet, toss potatoes, Brussels sprouts, and shallot with 1 Tbsp oil and ¼ tsp each salt and pepper. Arrange in single layer and roast 15 minutes.

Brush halibut with remaining ½ Tbsp oil and season with pinch each salt and pepper. Nestle into vegetables and roast until vegetables are golden brown and tender and halibut is opaque throughout, 12 to 15 minutes more.

PER SERVING: 385 cal, 37 g pro, 31 g carb, 7 g fiber, 4 g sugars (0 g added sugars), 13 g fat (2 g sat fat), 83 mg chol, 450 mg sodium

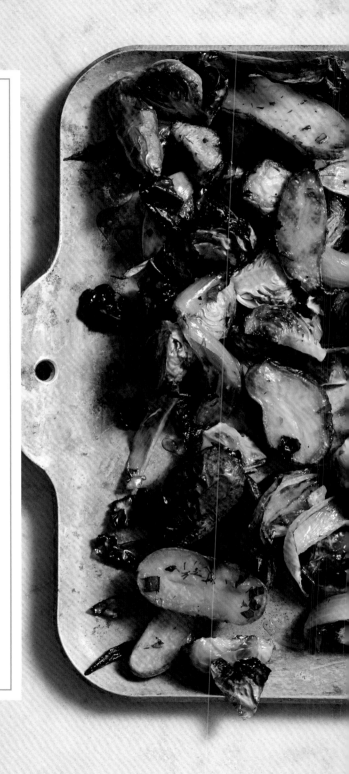

Fiery Black Bean Soup

This satisfying soup contains the perfect high-fiber and low-calorie combo, making it a great meal if you're trying to lose weight.

ACTIVE 45 MIN. | TOTAL 45 MIN. | SERVES 2

½ lb tomatillos (about 4), halved
2 cloves unpeeled garlic
1 large onion, cut into 1-in.-thick wedges
1 large poblano pepper, halved and seeded
1 jalapeño, halved and seeded
1 Tbsp olive oil
Kosher salt and pepper
½ tsp ground cumin
½ tsp ground coriander
4 cups low-sodium chicken broth
2 15-oz cans low-sodium black beans, rinsed
1 14.5-oz can fire-roasted diced tomatoes, drained
1 small red onion, thinly sliced
2 Tbsp fresh lime juice
Avocado chunks and cilantro leaves, for serving

Directions: Heat broiler. On large rimmed baking sheet, toss tomatillos, garlic, onion, poblano, and jalapeño with oil and ½ tsp each salt and pepper. Turn peppers cut sides down and broil, rotating pan every 5 minutes until vegetables are tender and charred, 15 minutes total.

Discard skins from poblanos and garlic. Finely chop vegetables and transfer to Dutch oven. Add cumin and coriander and cook on medium, stirring occasionally, 2 minutes. Add broth, beans, and tomatoes and bring to a simmer; cook 4 minutes.

Meanwhile, make pickled onion: toss red onion with lime juice and pinch each salt and pepper; let sit at least 10 minutes. Serve soup topped with pickled onion and cilantro.

PER SERVING: 325 cal, 20 g pro, 53 g carb, 18 g fiber, 8 g sugars (0 g added sugars), 6 g fat (1 g sat), 0 mg chol, 705 mg sodium

BONUS

BONUS

BONUS

BONUS

BONUS

RECIPES

Smoothie Bowls

Ditch the straw in favor of this heartier—but just as easy to assemble—version of a smoothie.

ACTIVE 5 MIN. | TOTAL 5 MIN. | SERVES 2

2 cups frozen raspberries
2 bananas
½ cup nonfat Greek yogurt
1 Tbsp chia seeds (optional)
½ cup low-fat milk
Granola, for serving
Toasted coconut flakes, for serving

Directions: In a blender, puree the raspberries, bananas, yogurt, chia seeds (if using), and milk until smooth.

Divide between bowls and top with granola and toasted coconut, if desired.

PER BOWL: 209 cal, 9 g pro, 46 g carb, 8 g fiber, 25 g sugars (0 g added sugars), 1 g fat (0.5 g sat fat), 3 mg chol, 49 mg sodium

Very Berry Quinoa Muffins

These light and healthy muffins get an extra hit of tart fruitiness from fresh raspberries.

ACTIVE 10 MIN. | TOTAL 30 MIN. | SERVES 12

¾ cup all-purpose flour, plus more for dusting
1 cup almond flour
¼ cup white quinoa (raw)
1 tsp baking powder
1 tsp ground cinnamon
½ tsp ground ginger
½ tsp baking soda
½ tsp kosher salt
2 large eggs, beaten
1 cup plain full-fat yogurt
¼ cup whole milk
⅓ cup honey
2 6-oz containers small raspberries
Toasted coconut flakes, for serving

Directions: Heat oven to 325°F. Lightly coat 12-cup muffin pan with cooking spray and dust with flour.

In large bowl, whisk together flours, quinoa, baking powder, cinnamon, ginger, baking soda, and salt.

In medium bowl, whisk together eggs, yogurt, milk, and honey. Fold egg mixture into flour mixture until just combined, then stir in raspberries.

Divide batter among muffin-pan cups and bake until toothpick inserted into centers of muffins comes out clean, 15 to 20 minutes. Cool in pan 5 minutes, then transfer to a wire rack to cool completely.

PER SERVING: 170 cal, 6 g pro, 23 g carb, 3 g fiber, 11 g sugars (8 g added sugars), 7 g fat (1 g sat fat), 34 mg chol, 205 mg sodium

Apple-Oatmeal Muffins

All the heart-healthy benefits of a bowl of oatmeal in a preppable, grab-and-go muffin.

ACTIVE 20 MIN. | TOTAL 40 MIN.
SERVES 12

2½ cups old-fashioned oats, divided
½ tsp freshly grated nutmeg
½ tsp ground cinnamon
½ tsp baking powder
½ tsp kosher salt
1 cup pecans, roughly chopped, divided
¼ cup olive oil
⅓ cup honey, warmed
2 large eggs
1 tsp pure vanilla extract
¾ cup unsweetened almond milk
2 Granny Smith apples, peeled and finely diced (2 cups total)
Toasted coconut flakes, for serving

Directions: Heat oven to 375°F. Line 12-cup muffin pan with cupcake liners and lightly coat with cooking spray.

In food processor, pulse 1 cup oats until very finely ground (should resemble coarsely milled flour); place in large bowl. Whisk in nutmeg, cinnamon, baking powder, and salt. Stir in half of pecans.

In medium bowl, whisk together oil and honey, then whisk in eggs, vanilla, and almond milk. Add egg mixture to oat mixture and mix to combine, then fold in apples and remaining 1½ cups oats.

Divide batter among muffin pan cups (about heaping ¼ cup each) and top with remaining pecans. Bake until tops no longer look shiny, 20 to 25 minutes.

PER SERVING: 225 cal, 4 g pro, 24 g carb, 3 g fiber, 11 g sugars (8 g added sugars), 13.5 g fat (1.5 g sat), 31 mg chol, 125 mg sodium

Chocolate-Cherry Granola Bars

Say hello to the perfect on-the-go breakfast. Make these at the beginning of the week for a sweet start to your morning.

ACTIVE 20 MIN.
TOTAL 30 MIN.
MAKES 14

2 cups old-fashioned oats

½ cup raisins

1 cup unsweetened dried cherries, divided

½ cup almond butter

¼ cup honey

¼ cup raw almonds, roughly chopped

½ cup dark chocolate chips

Directions: Heat oven to 350°F. Line an 8-in. square baking pan with parchment paper, leaving a 2-in. overhang on 2 sides.

Spread oats on a large rimmed baking sheet and bake until just golden brown, 8 to 10 minutes; let cool completely.

Meanwhile, place raisins and ½ cup cherries in a heatproof bowl. Cover with boiling water and let sit 10 minutes. Drain, transfer to a food processor, and puree until smooth. Add almond butter and honey and puree until smooth; transfer to a bowl.

Add oats and stir to coat, then fold in almonds, chocolate chips, and remaining ½ cup cherries. Pat mixture into the prepared pan and let set, about 1 hour.

Using the overhangs, transfer set mixture to a cutting board and cut into 14 bars.

PER BAR: 255 cal, 6 g pro, 29 g carb, 5 g fiber, 16 g sugars (8 g added sugars), 13 g fat (2.5 g sat fat), 0 mg chol, 10 mg sodium

Pumpkin-Cherry Breakfast Cookies

Who says you can't have cookies for breakfast? These are made with good-for-you ingredients, like whole-wheat flour and oats.

ACTIVE 15 MIN. | TOTAL 45 MIN.
MAKES 16 4-IN. COOKIES

2 cups whole-wheat flour
1 cup old-fashioned oats
1 tsp baking soda
1 tsp pumpkin pie spice
½ tsp kosher salt
1 15-oz can pure pumpkin
1 cup olive oil
1 cup brown sugar
1 large egg
½ cup roasted salted pepitas
½ cup dried cherries

Directions: Heat oven to 350°F. In a medium bowl, whisk together flour, oats, baking soda, pie spice, and salt.

Using an electric mixer, beat pumpkin, oil, sugar, and egg on medium to combine. Reduce speed to low; gradually incorporate flour mixture, then pepitas and cherries.

Scoop 16 mounds (about ⅓ cup each) onto parchment-lined baking sheets, spacing 2 in. apart; flatten into disks. Bake until dark brown on bottoms, 20 to 25 minutes. Transfer to wire rack to cool.

PER COOKIE: 290 cal, 4 g pro, 33 g carb, 3 g fiber, 16 g sugars (13.5 g added sugars), 16.5 g fat (2.5 g sat fat), 11.5 mg chol, 160 mg sodium

Tomato, Peach, and Basil Salad

This refreshing medley of summer flavors couldn't be easier to assemble.

**ACTIVE 10 MIN. | TOTAL 10 MIN.
SERVES 4**

- ½ **small red onion, thinly sliced**
- 1 **Tbsp red wine vinegar**
- **Kosher salt and pepper**
- 1 **lb heirloom tomatoes**
- 1 **lb yellow peaches or nectarines**
- 2 **Tbsp olive oil**
- ¼ **cup basil leaves**
- 2 **oz feta, broken into pieces**

Directions: In small bowl, combine onion and vinegar with ¼ tsp salt. Let sit 5 minutes.

Cut tomatoes and peaches into wedges and arrange on platter.

Stir oil into onion mixture and spoon over fruit, then sprinkle with basil, feta, and cracked black pepper.

PER SERVING: 75 cal, 2 g pro, 8 g carb, 2 g fiber, 12 g sugars (0 g added sugars), 4.5 g fat (1 g sat fat), 13 mg chol, 165 mg sodium

Smoky Chicken Soup

This warming soup fills you up with lots of protein and flavor.

ACTIVE 20 MIN. | TOTAL 20 MIN.
SERVES 4

1 onion, chopped
1 stalk celery, chopped
1 Tbsp olive oil
1 clove chopped garlic
6 cups low-sodium chicken broth
1 15-oz can hominy, rinsed
2½ cups cooked shredded white-meat chicken
1 Tbsp chopped chipotles in adobo
Chopped tomatoes, cilantro, and avocado, for serving

Directions: In a pot, sauté onion and celery in 1 Tbsp oil, covered, until tender. Stir in garlic; cook 1 minute.

Add chicken broth, hominy, chicken, and chipotles and bring to a simmer. Top with chopped tomatoes, cilantro, and avocado.

PER SERVING: 311 cal, 37 g pro, 24 g carb, 3 g fiber, 2 g sugars (0 g added sugars), 9 g fat (2 g sat fat), 74 mg chol, 485 mg sodium

Marinated Summer Squash Salad

Mixing quinoa into this fresh and crisp summer zucchini salad adds protein and helps you feel full.

ACTIVE 20 MIN. | TOTAL 50 MIN. (includes cooling)
SERVES 4

1 cup white quinoa
**2 lbs small zucchini, yellow squash,
or a combination (about 6 total)**
2 Tbsp olive oil
1 Tbsp lemon zest
2 Tbsp lemon juice
½ tsp Dijon mustard
Kosher salt and pepper
2 medium shallots, finely chopped
¼ cup flat-leaf parsley
¼ cup mint, torn
¼ cup toasted almonds, chopped
2 Tbsp crumbled feta

Directions: Cook quinoa per pkg. directions. Let cool 20 minutes.

Meanwhile, very thinly slice zucchini and squash lengthwise. In a large bowl, whisk together oil, lemon zest and juice, mustard, and ½ tsp each salt and pepper; stir in shallots.

Toss with zucchini and squash and let stand 5 minutes. Toss with cooked quinoa, parsley, mint, almonds, and feta.

PER SERVING: 335 cal, 12 g pro, 41 g carb, 8 g fiber, 8 g sugars (0 g added sugars), 15.5 g fat (2.5 g sat fat), 4 mg chol, 310 mg sodium

Warm Roasted Cauliflower and Spinach Salad

Pumpkin pie spice adds warmth to this easy vegetarian lunch.

ACTIVE 15 MIN. | TOTAL 40 MIN. | SERVES 4

3 Tbsp olive oil
1 tsp pumpkin pie spice
½ tsp ground cumin
½ tsp ground coriander
Kosher salt
1 small shallot
1 large head cauliflower, cut into florets (about 2 lbs)
1 14-oz can lentils, rinsed
3 Tbsp white wine vinegar
5 cups baby spinach
1 oz pecorino cheese, shaved
¼ cup pomegranate seeds

Directions: Heat oven to 425°F. In a small saucepan, warm oil, spices, and ½ tsp salt just until hot. Finely chop shallot and place in a small bowl. Pour half of oil mixture over shallot and set aside.

On a large rimmed baking sheet, toss cauliflower with remaining oil mixture and roast until golden brown and tender, 20 to 25 minutes.

Add lentils and vinegar to shallot mixture and let sit 5 minutes. When ready to serve, toss with spinach, pecorino, pomegranate seeds, and roasted cauliflower.

PER SERVING: 270 cal, 13 g pro, 29 g carb, 13 g fiber, 7 g sugars (0 g added sugars), 13 g fat (3 g sat fat), 7 mg chol, 435 mg sodium

Chickpea, Spinach, and Quinoa Patties

Chickpeas are a nutritional powerhouse; the little legumes pack protein, fiber, folate, and iron.

ACTIVE 15 MIN. | TOTAL 35 MIN. SERVES 4

¼ cup crumbled feta cheese
1 clove garlic
1 jalapeño, seeded
Kosher salt
½ cup packed baby spinach
2 scallions, quartered lengthwise, plus more for serving
½ cup cooked quinoa
1 15-oz can low-sodium chickpeas, rinsed
1 Tbsp olive oil
Mixed green salad, for serving

Directions: Heat oven to 425°F. In a food processor, pulse feta, garlic, jalapeño, and ¼ tsp salt until mostly smooth.

Add spinach and scallions and pulse a few more times to chop. Add quinoa and chickpeas and pulse to chop and combine.

Coat a rimmed baking sheet with oil. Scoop chickpea mixture into 2-Tbsp balls, transfer to baking sheet, and flatten slightly. Roast until bottoms are golden brown, 8 to 9 minutes. Flip and roast until other side is golden brown, 7 to 8 minutes more. Serve with mixed green salad.

PER SERVING: 180 cal, 8 g pro, 21 g carb, 5 g fiber, 3 g sugars (0 g added sugars), 7.5 g fat (2 g sat fat), 8 mg chol, 285 mg sodium

Cod with Crispy Green Beans

The ideal summer meal? Fast, flavorful, and fresh. This one checks all the boxes.

ACTIVE 20 MIN.
TOTAL 20 MIN.
SERVES 4

1 lb beans (green, wax or a combination)
2 Tbsp olive oil, divided
¼ cup grated Parmesan
Kosher salt and pepper
1¼ lbs skinless cod, cut into 4 pieces
2 Tbsp basil pesto

Directions: Heat oven to 425°F. On a large rimmed baking sheet, toss the beans with 1 Tbsp oil, then the Parmesan and ¼ tsp each salt and pepper. Roast until light golden brown, 10 to 12 minutes.

Meanwhile, heat the remaining Tbsp oil in a large skillet over medium-high heat. Season the cod with ¼ tsp each salt and pepper and cook until golden brown and opaque throughout, about 3 minutes per side; transfer to plates.

Spoon the pesto over the cod and serve with the beans.

PER SERVING: 242 cal, 21 g pro, 10 g carb, 3 g fiber, 4 g sugars (0 g added sugars), 11 g fat (2 g sat fat), 61 mg chol, 481 mg sodium

Zesty Shrimp with Chimichurri Rice

This herby dish comes together in less than 30 minutes, making it a perfect weeknight staple.

ACTIVE 25 MIN.
TOTAL 25 MIN.
SERVES 4

1 cup long grain rice
1 medium orange
1 cup fresh cilantro leaves
4 scallions sliced
2 cloves garlic
2 Tbsp olive oil, divided
¼ tsp crushed red pepper flakes
Kosher salt and pepper
1 lb peeled and deveined shrimp
½ tsp ground cumin
1 avocado

Directions: Cook the rice according to pkg. directions. Meanwhile, finely grate 2 tsp zest from the orange and set aside. Cut away the peel and white pith from the orange and, working over a large bowl, cut into segments. Roughly chop the segments and place into the bowl. Squeeze the juice from the membrane into the bowl, then mix in the cilantro, scallions, garlic, 1 Tbsp oil, red pepper flakes, and ¼ tsp salt.

Heat the remaining Tbsp oil in a large skillet over medium-high heat. Season the shrimp with the reserved zest, the cumin, and ¼ tsp each salt and pepper. Cook, tossing occasionally, until opaque throughout, 3 to 4 minutes.

Fold the rice and avocado into the chimichurri mixture and serve with the shrimp.

PER SERVING: 415 cal, 23 g pro, 53 g carb, 6 g fiber, 4 g sugars (0 g added sugars), 13 g fat (2 g sat), 135 mg chol, 331 mg sodium

Everything Bagel Crusted Salmon with Herby Fennel Salad

Everything spice blend (plus a squeeze of lemon!) provides fast flavor for flaky roasted salmon. Bright, crunchy fennel is the perfect pairing!

ACTIVE 20 MIN. | TOTAL 25 MIN. | SERVES 4

1½ lb skin-on salmon fillet
2 Tbsp olive oil, divided
Kosher salt and pepper
2 Tbsp everything spice blend
1 lemon
1 small bulb fennel, cored and very thinly sliced, plus ½ cup fennel fronds
3 scallions, thinly sliced
½ cup flat-leaf parsley leaves
½ cup cilantro leaves

Directions: Heat oven to 425°F. Place salmon, skin side down, on rimmed baking sheet and rub with 1 Tbsp oil, then sprinkle ¼ tsp pepper and all of everything spice on top. Thinly slice half of lemon and arrange around salmon. Bake until salmon is barely opaque throughout, 18 to 22 minutes.

Meanwhile, squeeze juice from remaining lemon half (about 1½ Tbsp) into medium bowl. Add fennel, remaining Tbsp oil and ¼ tsp each salt and pepper and toss to coat.

Just before serving, toss fennel with scallions, parsley, cilantro, and fennel fronds. Serve with salmon and lemon slices.

PER SERVING: 300 cal, 37 g pro, 8 g carb, 3 g fiber, 3 g sugars (0 g added sugars), 14 g fat (2.5 g sat), 80 mg chol, 330 mg sodium

Roasted Chili-Lime Drumsticks

With only five main ingredients, this dinner is both incredibly simple and amazingly delicious!

ACTIVE 15 MIN.
TOTAL 40 MIN. | SERVES 4

8 small chicken legs (about 1½ lbs)

Kosher salt and pepper

1 red onion, sliced (leave root intact)

1¼ lbs broccoli crowns, cut into florets

1 Tbsp chili paste (we used sambal oelek), plus more for serving

1 Tbsp olive oil

2 limes

Directions: Heat broiler. Pat chicken dry and season with ¼ tsp each salt and pepper. Place chicken legs and onion on a rimmed baking sheet and broil until browned, about 9 to 10 minutes. Remove baking sheet from oven and reduce oven temperature to 450°F.

While chicken broils, in a large bowl, toss broccoli with chili paste and oil.

Transfer broccoli to a second rimmed baking sheet and roast along with chicken until vegetables are golden brown and tender and chicken is cooked through, about 15 minutes.

Halve a lime and squeeze juice over chicken. Finely grate zest of other lime on top, then cut into wedges. Drizzle chicken with additional chili paste if desired and serve with lime wedges.

PER SERVING: 250 cal, 26 g pro, 13 g carb, 5 g fiber, 3 g sugars (0 g added sugars), 11.5 g fat (2.5 g sat fat), 113 mg chol, 325 mg sodium

Sticky Chicken with Scallion and Corn Rice

Give your go-to chicken and rice dinner a twist with this warming sauce and a mix of rice and scallions.

ACTIVE 20 MIN. | TOTAL 20 MIN. | SERVES 4

- **1 cup long-grain white rice**
- **1 cup frozen corn, thawed**
- **1 scallion, sliced**
- **1 Tbsp olive oil**
- **4 5-oz boneless chicken breasts**
- **¼ tsp ground ginger**
- **¼ tsp cinnamon**
- **Pinch ground cloves**
- **Pinch cayenne**
- **Kosher salt**
- **2 Tbsp honey**
- **2 Tbsp fresh lime juice**
- **½ tsp sesame seeds**

Directions: Cook the rice according to pkg. directions. Fold in the corn and scallion.

Heat the oil in a large skillet over medium heat. Season the chicken with the ginger, cinnamon, cloves, cayenne, and ¼ tsp salt and cook, about 5 minutes per side.

Drizzle with the honey and lime juice then sprinkle with the sesame seeds.

Serve with the rice and any pan juices.

PER SERVING: 347 cal, 29 g pro, 39 g carb, 2 g fiber, 11 g sugars (9 g added sugars), 8 g fat (1.5 g sat fat), 83 mg chol, 53 mg sodium

Roasted Sweet-and-Sour Brussels Sprouts

Aside from being high in heart-healthy fiber, Brussels sprouts also provide a dose of glucosinolates—compounds linked to lowering cancer risk.

ACTIVE 10 MIN.
TOTAL 35 MIN.
SERVES 4

1 lb Brussels sprouts, trimmed and halved
1 Tbsp olive oil
2 Tbsp reduced-sodium soy sauce
2 Tbsp balsamic vinegar
1 Tbsp brown sugar
¼ tsp ground ginger
Pepper
2 Tbsp flat-leaf parsley leaves, finely chopped

Directions: Toss together Brussels sprouts, oil, and 3 Tbsp water.

Line air fryer basket with piece of foil cut to fit. Add Brussels sprouts to basket and air-fry at 350°F, shaking basket twice, until golden brown and tender, 15 to 20 minutes.

Meanwhile, in 2-cup glass measuring cup, combine soy sauce, vinegar, brown sugar, ginger, and ⅛ tsp pepper. Microwave on High until syrupy, 2 to 2½ minutes.

Toss sprouts with parsley and enough sauce to coat. Serve remaining sauce on the side.

PER SERVING: 100 cal, 4 g pro, 15 g carb, 4 g fiber, 7 g sugars (3 g added sugars), 4 g fat (1 g sat), 0 mg chol, 315 mg sodium

Potato Salad with Red Onion Vinaigrette

Ditch the heavy dressing and opt for a zippy red onion vinaigrette for this fresh spring side, loaded with green peas and dill.

ACTIVE 15 MIN.
TOTAL 30 MIN.
SERVES 6

2 lbs baby yellow potatoes
Kosher salt and pepper
½ medium red onion, finely chopped
3 Tbsp white wine vinegar
3 Tbsp olive oil
1 tsp Dijon mustard
½ cup frozen peas, thawed
¼ cup fresh dill, roughly chopped

Directions: Place potatoes in medium pot and cover with cold water. Bring to a boil, add ½ Tbsp salt, reduce heat and simmer until just tender, 12 to 15 minutes.

Meanwhile, toss onion with vinegar and ½ tsp each salt and pepper and let sit, tossing occasionally.

Drain potatoes and run under cold water to cool. Drain well and pat dry, then halve any that are large.

Whisk oil and mustard into vinegar mixture. Add potatoes and toss to coat. Fold in peas and dill.

PER SERVING: 185 cal, 4 g pro, 30 g carb, 3 g fiber, 1 g sugars (0 g added sugars), 7 g fat (1 g sat fat), 0 mg chol, 310 mg sodium

Carrot and Radish Salad

Colorful carrot ribbons and thinly sliced radishes get dressed in a beautifully sweet-tart honey and citrus-juice lemon vinaigrette for the ultimate spring salad.

ACTIVE 25 MIN. | TOTAL 25 MIN. | SERVES 6

FOR VINAIGRETTE:
3 Tbsp fresh orange juice
3 Tbsp fresh lemon juice
1 tsp honey
Kosher salt and pepper
3 Tbsp olive oil
FOR SALAD:
4 mixed colored carrots, shaved lengthwise (about 3 cups)
4 radishes, shaved into rounds (about 1 cup)
2 stalks celery, thinly sliced (about 2 cups)
1 small beet, shaved into half-moon rounds (about 1 cup)
1 cup watercress
2 small oranges, rind removed and sliced into half-moons
½ cup fresh mint leaves, torn, if large

Directions: In bowl, whisk together orange juice, lemon juice, honey, and ½ tsp each salt and pepper to dissolve honey, then whisk in oil.

Arrange vegetables, oranges, and mint on large platter and drizzle with vinaigrette.

PER SERVING: 115 cal, 2 g pro, 13 g carb, 3 g fiber, 8 g sugars (1 g added sugars), 7 g fat (1 g sat), 0 mg chol, 235 mg sodium

White Bean and Cucumber Salad

Next time you need a quick fiber boost, whip up this crisp side dish.

ACTIVE 10 MIN. | TOTAL 10 MIN. | SERVES 8

¼ cup fresh lemon juice
3 Tbsp olive oil
1 tsp ground sumac
Kosher salt and pepper
2 15-oz cans low-sodium small white beans, rinsed
4 Persian cucumbers or ¾ seedless cucumber, thinly sliced
3 scallions, thinly sliced
¾ cup flat-leaf parsley, chopped

Directions: In a large bowl, whisk together lemon juice, oil, sumac, ¼ tsp salt, and ½ tsp pepper. Add beans and toss to coat, then toss with cucumbers and scallions. Fold in parsley.

PER SERVING: 155 cal, 6 g pro, 21 g carb, 6 g fiber, 2 g sugars (0 g added sugars), 5 g fat (0.5 g sat fat), 0 mg chol, 260 mg sodium

Turmeric-Roasted Beets with Orange Bell Pepper Romesco

In addition to bringing earthiness to this vibrant dish, turmeric lends an anti-inflammatory boost thanks to the curcumin it contains.

ACTIVE 10 MIN. | TOTAL 2 HR. SERVES 8

2 orange bell peppers, seeded and quartered
2 small tomatoes (we like Campari), halved
3 Tbsp olive oil, divided
Kosher salt and pepper
8 beets (about 1½ lbs), tops removed
1 tsp ground turmeric, plus more for serving
½ cup blanched almonds
1 clove garlic
1 Tbsp grated orange zest plus 2 Tbsp juice
1 Tbsp sherry vinegar
¼ cup flat-leaf parsley, finely chopped

Directions: Heat broiler. On a large rimmed baking sheet, toss peppers, tomatoes, 1 Tbsp oil, and ¼ tsp each salt and pepper. Broil, tossing once, until vegetables are tender and slightly charred, 8 to 10 minutes.

Transfer to a bowl and cover with plastic wrap. Set aside until cool. Carefully remove skins from peppers.

Reduce heat to 325°F. To a 9-in. square metal baking pan, add beets, turmeric, ½ cup water, 1 Tbsp oil, and ½ tsp each salt and pepper. Cover with plastic wrap, then foil. Roast until tender when pierced with a fork, 1 hour 30 minutes to 2 hours. Remove foil and plastic and, using a towel, carefully peel beets. Cut into wedges.

Transfer peppers and tomatoes to a food processor with almonds, garlic, orange juice, vinegar, and remaining Tbsp oil. Process until smooth. Fold in orange zest and parsley. Serve beets with half of romesco (refrigerate remainder for another use, up to 3 days) and dust with additional turmeric, if desired.

PER SERVING: 90 cal, 2 g pro, 8 g carb, 2 g fiber, 5 g sugars (0 g added sugars), 6 g fat (0.5 g sat fat), 0 mg chol, 195 mg sodium

Thank You for Purchasing
The Ultimate Heart-Healthy Full-Flavor Meal Plan

Visit our online store to find more great products from *Prevention* and save 20% off your next purchase.